# 666.... THE BEAST THAT LIES WITHIN

MIA W. JONES

Copyright ©2025 Mia W. Jones.

All rights reserved. No part of this publication may be reproduced, distributed or transmitted in any form or by any means, including photocopying, recording or other electronic or mechanical methods, without the prior written permission of the authors and/or publisher, except in the case of brief quotations embodied in critical reviews and certain other noncommercial uses permitted by copyright laws. For permission requests, write to "Attention: Permissions Coordinator", at the address below.
Redbaby Publishing, Inc.
8787 Branch Avenue, Unit 8
Clinton MD 20735

To contact the author for speaking engagements, email her at missioninaction228@gmail.com.

ISBN:
eBook 9781952163258
Paperback 9781952163265

2$^{ND}$ Edition – 2025

## Table of Contents

**Dedication**

**Preface**

**Playlist for 666 The Beast That Lies Within**

**Chapter 1: Introduction**

**Chapter 2: The Pretender**

**Chapter 3: Thunderstorms**

**Chapter 4: Fireworks**

**Chapter 5: Reading the Signs**

**Chapter 6: New Expectations**

**Chapter 7: Mixed Signals**

**Chapter 8: What is Narcissist Behavior**

Chapter 9: Predicaments

Chapter 10: The Devouring Stage

Chapter 11: Sabbatical

Chapter 12: The Encounter

Chapter 13: The Complete End of the Road

Chapter 14: Lessons

Chapter 15: And So It Was Ordered - Judgement

Chapter 16: Rise of the Phoenix

Chapter 17: The Birth of Raging War Ministries

Chapter 18: Discovery

References

About the Author

This book is not to destroy a person's character or personality, but it is written to show you what happens when you deal with a narcissist human being that is looking for ways to cope with their life as it is, instead of what it was. Wanting happiness and love all at the same time, but using its own ego, subjecting it on a person that only gives out empathy only to suck them dry, killing a person slow from the inside out.

People use this book as a tool to see and understand what narcissistic people can do to your mental, physical, and emotional state all at the same time. And for those of you that have been through it, you can relate in the same type of way, shape or form. Forgiveness, unconditional love, and patience for me was the lesson to be taught with this all.

After reading this book, what were the lessons you took from this madness?

Email me and tell me your story. Let me know how you made it through. If you are in a similar situation now, I am available to give words of wisdom.

This is dedicated to the one that needs embracement that is longing for just a touch from the Master Abba. Abba, thank you for the release to go to the next level in you. Peace and Blessings always loving with the Love of God,

Mia

## PreFace

The beginning of our relationship when everything was good. I truly believed that both of us were building a future together and bettering ourselves from past relationships. Some men do change, grow up and become that rock you need. And then some men …….

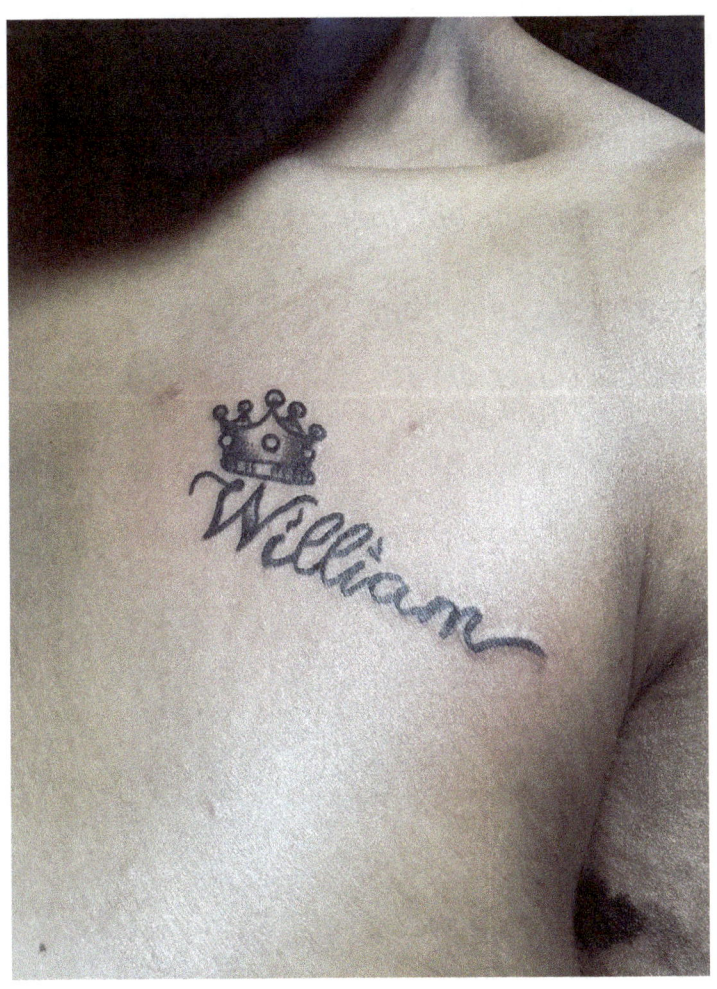

Songs of 666.... The Beast That Lies Within

Before sitting down to read this book, get yourself a nice glass of your favorite beverage or cocktail, load up this song list. As you read, let the words and melody take you into a deep dive of this romantic roller coaster ride. Enjoy!

## Introduction

- Donna Summer & Barbra Streisand – No More Tears (Enough is Enough)

## Pretender

- Chante Moore – It's Alright
- Ruben Studdard – Masterpiece
- Neyo – Good Man
- Neyo – Closer
- Neyo – Sexy Love

- *Beyonce f/Jay Z – Crazy Love*
- *Betty Wright – Clean Up Woman*
- *50 Cent f/Snoop Dog – P.I.M.P (explicit)*

Thunderstorms

- *Kelly Price – It's Gonna Rain*

Firework

- *R. Kelly – When A Woman's Fed Up*
- *Mary J Blige – My Life*
- *Monica – Superman*
- *Kanye West f/Jamie Foxx – Gold Digger*
- *Jaheim – Look for Love*
- *Johnny Nash – I Can See Clearly Now*

New Expectations

- *Jill Scott – Golden*
- *Megan Thee Stallion - Cobra*

- Ghetto Boys – Mind Playing Tricks On Me

- H-Town – Knockin' Da Boots

Mixed Signals

- Mary J. Blige – Real Love

- Beyonce – Irreplaceable

What is Narcissist Behavior

- Yung Bleu, Kehlani – Beautiful Lies

- Tems – Free Mind

- Melanie Fiona – It Kills Me

- Fat Joe, Remy Ma & French Montana – All the Way

- 2 Pac – Me Against the World

- Inayah – Best Thing

- Teddy Pendergrass – T.K.O.

- The Commodores – Sail On

Predicaments

- *Bradshaw and Roberson – Make Some Time*
- *Silk Sonic f/ Bruno Mars and Anderson Paak – Leave the Door Open*
- *Isley Brothers – Here We Go Again*
- *Johnny Gill – There You Go*

## The Devouring Stage

- *Bell Bid DeVoe – When Will I See You Smile Again*
- *Mariah Carey – Hero*
- *Wyclef Jean f/Mary J. Blige – 911*
- *Whitney Houston – Why Does it Hurt So Bad*
- *Rose Royce – Love Don't Live Here Anymore*

## Sabbatical

- *Rihanna – Rude Boy*

## The Encounter

- *Devon Gilfillian – The Good Life*

- *Soulja Boy – Crank That*

    The Complete End of the Road

- *Chris Brown – She Ain't You*

- *Donnell Jones – Karma*

- *Donnell Jones – Where I Wanna Be*

    Lessons

- *Eric Roberson – Lessons*

- *Queen Naija – Karma*

- *Mary J. Blige – Love Lesson*

    Rise of the Phoenix

- *Rose Royce – Love Don't Live Here Any More*

    The Birth of Raging War Ministries

- *Marvin Sapp – Teach My Hands to War*

# Chapter 1

## Introduction

In the summer of 2014, my world was tossed upside down. My marriage was in a shambles. Circumstances beyond my control left me and my two children, on the verge of being evicted. With little to no money, unemployed and no immediate help in sight, I was in dire straits. Throughout my life, my faith has always been a source of comfort, that one friend who has never failed me. I was living in Virginia. My ex-husband and I had started a small non-denomination church. One of the members from our congregation, Othello, befriended us and during my time of crisis came to my rescue, taking full advantage of the situation. And I do mean full advantage. I admit I was an emotional mess. But was it right to break my martial vows?

No of course not, but when you are vulnerable and craving for love, and affection, along with attention, you latch onto anyone and everyone who honestly gives you the time or day. He was saying all the right things, being the hero, I needed in the moment, and I was lapping it up. We became close over time, much closer than we should have, and I even expected. I should have known better, but I'm an optimist. I believe in giving people the benefit of doubt. I wholeheartedly believed what he was selling. Along with filling up the empty space with aspects of new dreams, I believed it. I had come to rely on him quite heavily. To some of you the flags may seem obvious. They were there screaming ATTENTION, like a drill sergeant with new prospects fulfilling their duties the whole time. I blindly saw them too. Things however blindly they may seem eventually come to the surface, blazing like a late summer day full of humidity tap dancing with a threat of colossal downpours.

People, as you read to grasp the details you will wonder what type of person does this to someone that they say they really love and care about? Should I have known better? YES! Should I have caught on? HELL YES! But I didn't. You will see as you read further that I did. I caught on to who he really was (the beast) that lays within. As if I was sleeping with the enemy. But it was a little too late. The damage was already done. I was already in too deep. Removing myself from one abusive relationship, and into another, here I go again. This here situation, not! No, no, no, no, no! Enough is enough (D. Summer & B. Streisand)!

## Chapter 2

## The Pretender

Othello became my lifeline at that point. We were in constant contact with each other. To be completely honest, I was alright with it (Chante Moore). I enjoyed the draw to him, like I was his masterpiece (Ruben Studdard). He was rebuilding this clay of a mess I found myself in. His attentiveness as a good man (Neyo), luring me closer (Neyo) and constant intimacy. Initially, it was cute and comforting, "Are you and the kids, okay?" to the nagging, "When are you going to make time for me?" Then the phone calls started about Alicia. He asked me if his wife was calling and asked me all types of questions about what was going on with us. He would call and text me, giving me the rundown, letting me know she was on to our communicating. It looked suspicious to her. So now he's lying to Alicia and asking me to co-sign for him about the deceit and lies. I did not intend to break my marriage vows. I take marriage and commitment seriously, but after all my husband had put me through, I'm human just like everyone else. My mindset at the time was I needed some crazy love (Beyonce), attention, and affection as well. That one false move, though, led to everything else forthcoming.

I just didn't want to see it. I wasn't trying to feel any hurt from another person yet again, either. But there I was, the cleanup woman (Betty Wright), cleaning up his mess when I wasn't the one that started it. But I did allow it!

So, I got tied up and entangled with a man that I thought really cared about me. I fell hard, and there's nothing I would not do for him at this point. I'm sure that the enemy blindsided me, and it was with everything that concerned him, but I was blind to everything all around me as well. Every red flag waving right in front of my face. My blinders were on, and I ignored every one that was waving all in my face. With limited options and feeling rejected by my husband, I moved back to Maryland to be with my family. Family is everything to me, and I knew that if I was having a rough time, I could go home. So, that is what I did.

I stayed in touch with Othello. My sister Maxine is trying to reason with me to find out why was I continuing my relationship with Othello. That was my first fatal mistake in not listening to her. My sister says to me, "You will not continue to be doing that mess while living in my house. Ungodly things in my home are not allowed, and if this is something that you want to do (giving me a choice), then you must go." And that is exactly what I did, because I wanted to continue whatever I had going on that was fulfilling my needs at that time. My sister doesn't stand for any foolishness. And she wasn't taking nothing from me even as a grown adult. She raised all six of us in the church. For her, it's holiness or hell. It was taught to us, we had free will to choose which way we want to go. No, she did not agree with nor condone my decision. She raised us up the best way she could, but at the point of age of understanding. She knew that the way we took the sin was not on her. So, telling us the right way was all she could do. There would be no hard feelings if I kept in touch and as long as she knew I was safe, then she was fine.

And while this transition was going on from Maryland, I couldn't control my mind and it was always overthinking. I was always on the go either to find a job, housing or any other business that needed to be taken care of. I could not keep still. Along with all that I kept my relationship with Othello. I drove down to Virginia every chance I could. Traveling from Maryland to Newport News, which is known for bad news. That should have been a sign for me. God gives us signs all around us for us to see and take advantage of. All that time all he was imparting caution signs, and I didn't even realize.

Now people, I bet you are wondering, if this man was seeing another woman because his wife is out of town, and I live in Maryland. That is too much space for him not to be doing his thing." Indeed, you are correct. Of course, he did! Now the P.I.M.P 50 Cent wrote about has made himself known, and very well I might add. Come on now. A man that is all about the love of himself. Of course, he is getting it in. I just didn't know about it at that time. It wasn't revealed yet. My head was stuck so far up his tail I couldn't see nothing but his love bombing that he was doing at the time, which was dicking me down for great pleasures. All I knew in my mind it was me and me alone, that he cared about and wanted to be with me, because his wife wasn't fulfilling her duties. How about them apples? What a mind frame to have about someone else's husband!

December 2014, I experienced an unexpected hospitalization. My kids and I had just come into the house from a long walk. I picked up the phone to call my ex-husband to deliver some bad news regarding his case. The judge had denied him release to come home early. Shortly after the conversation ended, I fell to the floor and began convulsing. Panicked, my son ran to get help. It was unknown at the time what was happening to me. While hospitalized, I suffered from several more episodes where my body was convulsing. The doctors found that the cause of the convulsions resulted from a brain injury suffered at the hands of my ex-husband. Yeah, the beating that I took before the arrest caused me to battle with epileptic and non-epileptic seizures from his wrath.

But Othello, who was supposed to be there, the love of my life. My guardian angel. The man I thought loved me.

Do you think he cared enough to check on me or to see if anything has happened to me? Naw, that seems to be normal for him reflecting on it now. I wasn't the first that he did that too, and surely will not be the last because that seems to be his MO. I was in the hospital for one month and on the verge of dying. My thoughts? He ghosted me. No phone calls, no visits. What the HELL is going on. If he cared so much for me, he would have tried all means to get in contact with me, any means necessary.

## Chapter 3

## Thunderstorms

Moving forward with dealing with Othello, I didn't see the pattern developing. He was always trying to stay one step ahead of me. One day I'm going to church from Garrett County to Baltimore with one of the young adults in the church. I'm driving and it was raining hard that day (Kelly Price). During this time, Othello and I were conversing while I was in route. Somewhere in the conversation we disagreed, and he began to talk about me and my looks, and his dumb tail began comparing me to his baby's mother. He then makes a statement: "Do you think you look better than my babies' mothers?", trying to attack my confidence. I didn't care what he said either way; they didn't look better than me in my opinion. One thing is for certain: my self-esteem wasn't that low, that I would allow his or anyone else's negative statements to define me. So, at that point, he felt the need to gaslight me and sent me Toya's picture, the one that he considers got away, and then somehow could regain ground for him to allow her to make a debut at a point of needing to be attended to at that point in his life. And with that began a repetitive cycle because of being damaged goods. With that being said, People, realize this about me. I am never going to say to any man that I don't look good just because you feel another woman in your eyes is better looking. Nigga please, if you had the guts to send me that picture, I'm assuming that you still wanted her or still had feelings for her. In my opinion though, I'm wondering why you continue to give her a bad rep.

So, when I received the text, I ran off the road into the middle ravine. Crazy old me in a rage. I was like, what the HELL! This nigga had some nerve to do some bull crap like that. It's raining hard, and I keep getting in and out of the car, getting wetter and wetter by the minute. All I could think about was one motto: "I am sugar, and just like sugar, I melt." About this time, I am standing outside waiting on a tow truck, all the while trying to get unstuck from the dirt and grass, along with big puddles of water. It had me sitting and waiting there for four hours. I felt fired up and ready to go in disgust, waiting to get unstuck, thinking about my next steps, and how I was going to get him back. And even at that moment, I can recall that he didn't care either. At that point, I made up my mind about what the point was. So, I stopped all communication. It was like a cease – and - desist took place. But really, what did I learn from it, I don't know really, because I was still yearning for more even though I knew it would not change the narcissistic behavior.

## Chapter 4

## Fireworks

When you first meet a person, what catches your eye? Is it the person themselves? Honestly, men. Is it their personality? Or is it their eyes, or the clothes that they are wearing? Or just maybe it's their body – the breast, legs? That female caress, print, from their vagina, or is it that buttocks that hits the target? If you are a female scoping out a male, Ladies! Is it the print, that package, you see between the legs? Or maybe it's his outfit, the car he's driving, or how his six-pack shows under a white wifebeater. Whatever it is, something must attract you to the person that you enter a relationship with.

When I met Othello, my life wasn't what it seemed to be from the outside. He never knew initially because I played the role of a dutiful wife, as the Bible says I should. Only God and a few of my family members knew my pain. R. Kelly says it best in his infamous song *When A Woman's Fed Up*. And that I was to the utmost.

My ex-husband was wallowing deep in some mess at the time, catching me off guard. He had anger issues to boot, and I often found myself as his punching bag during those times. Don't get it twisted; I can land a few of my own. There was never an innocent bystander between him and me. But, he was the breadwinner of the home, so I had to acknowledge him as such, being the woman who was the stay-at-home parent. I believe, and still do to this day, that marriage is a covenant. You should do everything in your power to make it work. Right? I met Othello through him. One day after work, he brought him by for a meet and greet. I took a deep breath. He introduces him as a single father with two kids who live with him.

I will not lie; he caught my eye, the very first moment I saw him. He was handsome, but that wasn't what drew me to him. At that moment, I felt a draw to him, as if we had already met before or in another lifetime. He was here just for me, to save little old me. Here I am married, yet this man had such a draw on my soul, like we were soulmates destined to spend our lives together. Now, at this point, I had a moment of *Come to Jesus*. God, what is happening to me? It's wrong for me even to be feeling this way. This right here is the last thing I need. I'm already going through Hell and this drama will only drive me deeper. Two wrongs don't make it right. I can only be held accountable for my actions. So, I need to be a good girl.

From that point on, they became good friends through learning and understanding the word of God, through the breakdown of how my ex-husband would teach it. Othello found it very interesting. When two people get along well, they usually have a lot of common interests and understanding. At that point, I should have realized that these two had similarities that drew them to one another. They say birds of a feather flock together. I should have put two and two together. All the signs were on the wall before me, but I didn't. That is why I ended up where I did at that point.

As time passed, I found information about him through my ex-husband as he was venting his problems to him for advice and relief. I didn't see a problem because that's what married folks do. They have pillow talk. They share information about their lives to get a handle on what they can't truly understand, so they look for an outsider to be an inside voice to give reason. It seems that Othello had a girlfriend. I was stunned, almost disappointed, when I learned about her and everything Othello was doing for her. Never seen anything like that. It was as if she had kryptonite. As we all know which is what takes Superman out of the game. In my eyes Othello was precisely that, Superman.

    God says we should not be envious, but Othello had a relationship with her that I longed to have with my ex-husband at that point in my life. I just knew I was a far better woman to receive better than what I was getting. I continued to listen, and I said to myself, "Wow. Is it love there or is she just a female gold digger?" I'm sitting back watching the lyrics play out, but to the fullest extent on the flip side.

    As time passed, we became more acquainted due to Othello becoming a church member, and sometimes she would accompany him. Moving forward, Othello and she decide to get married. He said that she proposed to him. Wow! He was so excited and proclaimed that she was the one for him. Hey, I won't judge because in the 21st century that is what some ladies may not look for anymore. Tradition seems to be going out the window. I'm just saying belief or not, on each of their own. This relationship between Othello and her was an on, off again thing. Over time, I realized they were two peas in a pod at least in my eyes. They had so many similar qualities. Unbeknownst to me, he was dating two women at the time, Alicia, and Odessa, and eventually he chose Alicia to be his wife since Odessa ghosted him, not knowing that he thought of her to be the one at that point in his life, but she missed out, he stated.

    Amidst all this, God gave me a word to share with them: that they would be good together and that their marriage would last, contingent on putting God first. God prophesied other things to me, but I kept it private. You can't tell some people anything they are not ready to hear. Some things must be discovered on their own. Gifts are without repentance, so God still used me even in this. Seemingly, when you don't have a background of Christianity or faith to build a foundation upon, it was hard for her to believe the words that were coming out of my mouth. After that happened, over time, I found out whether they had a field day talking about me. "Some prophetesses? I can only imagine how many areas of the house it hit before it got a great laugh. I wonder...was it the bedroom or dining room? Maybe it was the living room or not, or the car. But, okay, whatever." I spoke God's truth. It was up to them to take it seriously or not.

Moving forward to the day they got married. No parents, children, or friends showed up. Nobody was there to see the matrimony but my family. We were members of the church. I thought it was odd, but then again, it was just about them and maybe that's how they wanted it.

Right after the wedding, not even two months after Othello and I wed, all HELL broke loose in my household. My then husband got convicted of a crime, and I found myself in dire straits. No money, about to be homeless, no job, and absolutely nothing was going right. You heard right, no; no; nada, zilch. All I can listen to over and over in my mind is tell me that we are going to be okay?

Here I am with nothing. I get home and find out we're being evicted. What in the world? Silly me, to think he would at least have been truthful with me and collaborated to ensure that the kids and I would be okay, right? We lost everything: our home, cars, and the church he founded. There was no such thing as stability for me at least as I knew of it. When this happened, I didn't know what to do at all. I didn't know where to go, who to call, or who to turn to about this. My mind went blank. At some point that night, I called the family on both sides and our spiritual parents, then at the time, to let them know what had happened in court.

Days before I talked to him about making plans because God had revealed to me that he was going to jail. He didn't want to believe it. So, we got into an argument, and things got heated, and he took his anger out on me.

Right after that, my sister Maxine called and talked to me. She told me what God had told her, which happened to be the same thing I stated to my ex-husband at the time. I gave him the phone so she could say to him as well.

At this point, he was thinking about ways to tell the judge why he couldn't go to jail, which was the truth, but the judge wants him to pay for his actions because they happened in the state of Maryland before we got married, which I was unaware of because of his omission.

I also called Othello to let him know what had happened. He came to the house as if he would rescue me and the children. When he came, he brought his boys to help and offered me his credit card for food and shelter. I thought it was nice of him. I asked him about his wife. He said that she didn't want to come. Othello was there every step of the way for the next few weeks, even months. I cannot tell you how grateful I was in those moments. I appreciated him and everything that he was doing throughout the process of the situation. I told myself he is doing a lot that he doesn't even have to do. *"This is truly a blessing, but was it a disguise to cover up something deeper that he didn't want anyone to discover."*

What I had to go through because of an irresponsible person was pure torture. We became closer through conversation while breaking down the church, leading to our intimacy over time. I was reeling from all the hurt of my husband's indiscretions and faults. Othello was there in every sense that another man can be, leaving no space for negativity with all that was going on. He was always trying to brighten my day in some way.

But, by me still married, and I am sleeping with a man that doesn't even belong to me. It became an unbreakable soul tie by sleeping with the person, which is bound to put you in bondage. And the type of bondage you don't know, and you will never see it coming. Just know when you're not in line by God's word, destruction awaits you. Come on now, people.

Spending a lot of time with Othello made me fall into a place of vulnerability that I never wanted with him. Jaheim says it best: *looking for love in all the wrong places, being around, and seeing a lot of pretty faces*. It gives space to the enemy. Many one-on-one talks and time spent managing the business of closing the church can be very consuming. All this had led me to fall hard for a married man. I told myself it was none of my business in his household between him and his wife, but her leaving to do LPN duty in different states puts him in a promiscuous state. Little did I know that it was always the nature of Othello to stray from promised vows and commitments.

Cheating when you are in a marriage varies; all three emotions can come into play, physically, emotionally, and mentally. Either way, your mind isn't on your partner or God. It started emotionally, as he supported the children and me, ensuring we were good. I thought, wow, I never saw a man that would be there as a friend. See, that was the bribe, because he was already sizing me up with the clothes that I was wearing, gray fitted sweatpants that revealed my shape, and I most certainly looked good in them. I'm not even noticing that I'm the next prey on his list. I always look good in anything and everything that I put on. And for him to be my ex-husband's friend, his eyes shouldn't have even traveled my way. But mine shouldn't have been either.

Everything was coming to a head for me. I felt like I was losing everything: my marriage, the church, our home, and my sanity. I couldn't even focus on being a mom correctly to our children, but I managed enough to keep my sanity and them afloat. While breaking down the church, I was steadily venting, and Othello was more than eager to listen. By him and I having venting sessions, we grew closer. During that conversation, I mentioned that I was still looking for a place to stay. Without blinking an eye, his vision clear (Johnny Nash), he put me and my children in a hotel. That was cool but understand this woman always finds out what a man's motives are before getting involved in solicitation. The day had been so humbling, so I took the help that was offered. My kids and I went to the hotel. That night, I was happy, and my children had a place to lay their heads. At that moment, it was a breath of fresh air. I must say, to get some sleep and get my thoughts together for my next move in this horrific ordeal of a situation. It was an exhale moment.

    He came to see us the following day. I was finishing up my daughter's hair and lying in bed watching TV with no thoughts of doing anything else but resting. Othello crawled into the bed next to me and started feeling me up, wanting to have sex with me. I was vulnerable, wanting a man's touch, and he was available and so was I. So, we did. It didn't last long, and it wasn't anything to talk about, but the moment was pleasurable enough to take away the thoughts of all that was happening at that time. It wasn't on my mind to do it, it just happened out of the blue.

## Chapter 5

## Reading the Signs

A few months back in Maryland I ended up in the hospital for several days. I'm finally being released from the hospital, still recovering from the scare of my life. Where's Othello? My phone number was still active, so he had the means to reach out. My family knew about him. They would have updated him about my conditions. So, if he cared so much, why didn't he call? Why didn't he come to see me? I was in so much physical and emotional pain. Going through that, it took a toll on my body, and along with work on my mind, as well as dealing with physical pain, my mind was all over the place.

I was on a mission to get to my family to let them know I was okay. And God delivered me out of the hands of death on a mission just to please God in the newness, but I still had a desire and longing for presence for Othello. So, I drove to Newport News just to be comforted in the moment by a man I was over the moon for. Only to underestimate his responses to the way I looked to him. It was hurtful to me, but I never expressed it. When I saw him, I didn't look the same. I had lost weight. My head was covered with a knitted hat. I wear it because I needed something soft to the touch on my head due to all the pain. My hair came out due to shock treatments that I was getting. I just recalled him looking at me differently. You would have thought he would have been saying, "I miss you. Where have you been? Is everything okay? I love you! Something that you say to someone when you haven't seen them for a long time. His take was I was M.I.A. He eventually said it, but it wasn't the first thing that came out of his mouth, and neither did I feel that it was heartfelt. But in my mind, I thought he thought if he gave me a quick *hit sexually, that it would* clear my aches and pains. At that moment I longed for hands to caress my body. But what did it do for me but keep blinders on to the real him. At that moment, his charisma was soaping me up, and I was getting too deep. No matter the cost, it was a desire I had to receive to justify why I was there in the first place. I could have let him go from when we weren't in contact with each other anyway. But you know me, I opened a can of worms just to give me an itch that only he could scratch. I didn't want to acknowledge it though. This is the person who I thought loved me. It would seem only right to feel that you're the only one in his life. This is what he was telling me. I was sadly mistaken.

    I dismissed it, and I'm rebuilding my life, working and living in Maryland. Traveling to Newport News every opportunity I get to spend time with Othello. I had gotten sick again with endometriosis and didn't know about it. Sex was painful. Cramping was even worse and the smell of blood from intense menstrual cycles was driving me insane. Him as well, with a great laugh of having s*** on his dick. Lord, that was a time right there. The doctors were informing me that I would need to have a hysterectomy to get the situation under control. It most definitely wasn't the news that I wanted to hear. Curiously, I asked Othello if he would like to father my fourth child. This was something that I had always wanted and desired. My husband could not do this due to his situation at the time. And I wanted to have another opportunity to have another child. My prognosis from the doctors was to the point that I would be unable to birth anymore children. Othello and I were building a life together, at least I thought we were. So, asking him about this was only natural. First, he agreed. I was happy and thought, "woman, you are still married, and your husband is locked up." He came back over time with the answer that sounds a little like this, "It just won't work with both of us being married. Of course, by now you have gotten the picture that we spent so much time investing in each other, in every way, which has brought us to the point. Yup, we fell in love, or so he said during this time.

But you know I should have known something was up. I was always running or doing something when it pertained to him. To my belief, there's a saying "nothing in this world is free," and I guess I was paying for the help all along, never knowing that he had other side chicks giving him affirmations and acts of service; he's leaving his venom of manipulation with all of us. We are spending time together regaining the time that we lost. We're talking on the phone. I think everything is grand. Here, I think I was alone, fulfilling the needs of a man in the same situation I was in, but I wasn't alone cleaning up what another woman dished out. Othello is a doozy. He said he loved me but only to an extent. This is, and has always been, his verbal language. People can say things they don't mean, or the knowledge of understanding that people's feelings and emotions are involved. That's why I was sadly mistaking a man for a boy and trying to work out his inner child. With that, I had seen all that, missed the Red Flags, dismissed it, and began rebuilding my life. I believed we still had a chance.

## Chapter 6

## New Expectations

In the NIV, Romans 16:17-19, *I urge you, brothers, and sisters, to watch out for those who cause divisions and put obstacles in your way that are contrary to the teaching you have learned. Keep away from them. For such people are not serving our Lord Jesus Christ, but their own appetites*, and Proverbs 18:12, *Before destruction a man's heart is haughty, but humility comes before honor.*

From these two scriptures alone, I should have gained a little wisdom and discernment of what I was getting myself into, but because of my desire that overlooked what my spirit told me. Knowing the person who I saw, Othello to be loving, kindhearted, sensual, understanding, free spirited and always thought of himself in high regard. At least that is what I want to remember best about him. So, a few years have passed and I'm on Facebook. He leaves a post on my page, and I respond. I had forgotten all about why we stopped talking in the first place. Oh, how I was a fool, a fool over flesh and not spirit.

So, I responded, and we began to get reacquainted after all the years of being apart from one another. In my mind a woman wants what she wants. I had told Othello that I don't deal with men on a friendship level because they are most often wanted more than what I have to offer. I told him if I talk to you, we can talk about moving into a relationship or don't waste my time. As we spoke, I am multitasking too many things that I had in mind for myself. Accomplishing them was first and foremost. I was not in the business of selling myself short for no man.

I went wrong, putting myself out there and having expectations that he was going to respect what I said. It wasn't like he didn't know what I had gone through and even the events after. Why subject a woman to more burdens that she wasn't willing to bear, let alone carry anymore. So, Othello said yes, he understood and proceeded to move on with a friendship that led into a relationship. I thought that it was great starting off. Prior to this relationship coming into existence, I came into a nice amount of funds after my divorce and said that I was good to make do for me and my family, as well as be a blessing to those that are in need. If you ask anyone about me, they will tell you that I am a helper from one to another. If I got it to give, I surely will with no hesitation even if it was my last. Hardworking and saving pays off when you are put in desperate situations. I have done it time and time again.

So, what I did wrong was tell Othello what I had after the fact of giving him two thousand dollars right off the break to get a tree cut down from in front of his home. Along with purchasing phones for my family and his mother trying to save funds paying to different cellphone companies. Remember the expectation that I had in the beginning. He heard me but he already set in his mind what I was going to be in his life prior to contacting me and as you read you will see why. No, Othello didn't ask me in the beginning to do any of the things that I did. But I had already set in my mind that I was going to give him whatever his heart desired because I was already head over hills for him. I couldn't do anything but remember how he went out of his way to make sure that me and my children were good in our time of need. People, in my mind I felt like those type of people were hard to come by and I never want to miss out on someone as great as he was to me and my kids. So, I thought.

About three months in he said to me, 'I think that this is a little too much for me. We are going to have to stop this right here." I didn't want to end it, but I am not the one to just sleep around either. If you're going to commit to me, this long-term relationship should lead to marriage or nothing at all. It's easy for a beautiful woman like me to get a man, but when I have choices, I want what I want; point blank period. This woman is very picky of who I have for keeps. I am an over the moon, shoot for the stars type of woman, and with that being said I fall hard. It's NO POINT that I am all about the one that I'm with and most definitely the world is going to know I am sold out for the man of. But in this case, it was a half off sale. And it was something that he couldn't handle from his words and his actions along the way. We had already had conversations about what I expected going back into this relationship with me. A few days later I go over to his house to chill and talk. I ask him about marriage because after all I'm not going to be with anyone long term and it doesn't lead to it. I'm just not that type of woman. I treat my butterfly like it's *golden* (Jill Scott, in that very shape, form and fashion. Baby let's not get it twisted.

So, he begins to say straight up with no hesitation, "Marissa we not getting married. You rush in this all too fast for me and I think we should slow down." And in my mind, I'm reeling like, *you did remember what I said right? So why did you even come back? What was your purpose for coming back or trying to reconnect knowing my thoughts and feelings, who I am and what we already did and what we been through together? I clearly said I hear you, but this is the beginning of our relationship so why would I expect that from you now, feeling as though we were picking up from where we left off? So many times. Why else a man keeps coming back is the reason for laying down the law in the beginning. At some point you must have understood that marriage is the end game for me. You know this right?*

Honestly, I can say we both were two direct people and we both were going to make our points known on what we were feeling. I'm thinking all at the same time. I can't say my point of view was understood or heartfelt. His on the other hand, I beg to differ. But me, I should have started to question who, what, when where and why. I didn't pay any attention to the first RED flags waving at me the first time. Like I said, all I could see and remember is I'm going to strike like a cobra (Megan Thee Stallion). That is what I knew him to be in my head. My mind played tricks on me as Ghetto Boys rap. Looking back at that moment, I felt that my heart was going to be shattered, but I paid it no mind. I continued the weekend. It was memorable and that it was, but not the way I expected. But he said his peace and I said mine and went on about the day. Othello, *knockin' da boots* as H Town croons. Trouble is a coming.

    The love bombing phase is incredible as if the Hulk was in this room making his presence known. Going from his humanly gentleman to a green monster busting out of his clothes and wondering if Tarzan was still ruling the jungle, or in the jungle. Othello knew how to set the mood from start to finish. I never seen a male that knew how to win you over with a home cook meal. With a little smooth talk to get you in the mood. Where you are like on edge, and you are waiting for a race to begin. Ready, set, go. Got you saying your ABCs and 123s. And having your head spin like the lady on death becomes her.

With all that about the third time, I was hooked from beginning to end because I knew what I was getting every time without fail. Honestly, it never was a disappointment. The right lighting, music, touch from head to toe. He moves me right to left, up and down, and then he makes me turn around. But with all that I have no "control" in the intimacy either. He did everything, every time. Hmm, one day I took the time to ask when I was going to have some play into how this goes Sir! Like what! Never in my life did I deal with that in a sexual encounter, nor understood it. But of course, I went along with it because my need was getting met either way. I had no complaints about it, so I let it continue. The show must go on as people would say.

# "Take care of your business"
# − $300

Social activity

 0     0

Status
Complete

Payment method

**Visa Debit**
Debit •••• 7476

Transaction details
June 19, 2021 9:40 AM · 🔒 Private

# "Take care of your business"
# − $2,000

## Social activity

 0    0

---

## Status
Complete

## Payment method
**Visa Debit**
Debit •••• 7476

## Transaction details
June 8, 2021 4:09 PM · 🔒 **Private**

## "Tire"
## - $220

Social activity

 0     0

---

Status
Complete

Payment method

**Visa Debit**
Debit •••• 7476

Transaction details
October 7, 2021 1:33 PM · 🔒 Private

## "Because I love you"
## - $225

Social activity

 0     0

---

Status
Complete

Payment method

**Visa Debit**
Debit •••• 2989

Transaction details
September 29, 2021 4:49 PM · 🔒 Priv

"Ride home"
# − $100

Social activity

 0     0

Status
Complete

Payment method

**Visa Debit**
Debit •••• 2989

Transaction details
September 23, 2021 11:33 AM · 🔒 Pı

# "Whatever you need it for"
# - $100

## Social activity

 0     0

## Status
Complete

## Payment method

 **Visa Debit**
Debit •••• 7476

## Transaction details
August 24, 2021 12:32 PM · 🔒 Private

## "Fixing our computer"
## - $200

#### Social activity

 1     1

---

#### Status
Complete

#### Payment method

 **Visa Debit**
Debit •••• 7476

#### Transaction details
August 26, 2021 12:18 PM · 🔒 Private

## "Flight"
## - $200

**Social activity**

 0     0

---

**Status**
Complete

**Payment method**

 **Visa Debit**
Debit •••• 7476

**Transaction details**
September 9, 2021 6:29 AM · 🔒 Priva

"Flight"
## - $50

Social activity

 0   0

---

Status
Complete

Payment method

**Visa Debit**
Debit •••• 7476

Transaction details
September 9, 2021 5:08 PM · 🔒 Priva

# "Service for the Car"
# - $600

**Social activity**

 0     0

---

**Status**
Complete

**Payment method**

VISA  **Visa Debit**
Debit •••• 7476

**Transaction details**
October 22, 2021 1:50 PM · 🔒 Private

## Chapter 7

## Mixed Signals

Even during our talks about marriage, he was giving me mixed signals, but I played that off too, with two failed marriages on his part, and two failed marriages on mine. Who wouldn't have cold feet? We talked about it all the time, and he's sending me pictures of rings to find out which ones I like. We even spent time shopping for them as well. But, when he gets around others, the story becomes different. He was just leading me on if I do say so myself. He had moments when he would confide in me about his relationships with other women and the petty things he did. I continued to hear these things even though I had questions, and as I did, I got answers that I needed to know, which caused an argument that wasn't even necessary.

Because I felt that it was his past and didn't have anything to do with me, it did because his acts were a continual repeat in every relationship that he had, which varies by person and the way they saw the relationship experience. I want real love, as (Mary J Blige) would imply. Is that just too much to ask for? I am unsure *why you would continue to do the same at your age. Now don't you think it's played out like an eight track for God's sake. Grow up and get some actual balls. Be a man and not a boy. Man, up Jack! March to the left and get it right because you know in your heart that I'm irreplaceable (Beyonce).*

    Let's not forget about the financial aspect of this situation. Funds that were given freely from my heart for nothing in return. The expectation was to build a life with him. I called myself planting seeds into what I wanted the outcome to be, living off of biblical principles. The children and I moved to North Carolina, hoping to become a blended family. But all the while he knew that he wasn't relocating. So, he told me what he needed to do before relocating. And that was to handle his business in Virginia and then move to North Carolina to be with me. That was the plan. He was still making trips back to Virginia. He constantly told me that he was getting things right to move.

All the while I found a place, a single-family home in Gastonia. At first, we were told the place would be ready in a month. Then the leasing office informed us they required additional work, which involved remodeling. While waiting for this house, we were living out of hotels one after another, which was significantly costly and started to add up. I became fed up with all the delays from the leasing office. I told Othello "Something has to give. I moved to be with you so that we can be a family. You are going to help me find another place." After a lot of arguing, he agreed. I didn't expect him to come through. He may have felt I forced him to help me, yet he decided we were a committed couple. I found us an apartment to rent with him providing the funds for us to move in but had to pay him back (smh). He moved our stuff into the apartment. I was again grateful because I was tired of not being in my place. But, at the same time, the apartment became a flat-out mess in the long run. Every time I would complain, he would say you picked.

    My Lord, it was bug-infested because others were filthy. Every time you stepped out of the door, there was dog poop everywhere. The smell just made us want to gag. No matter how often I sprayed the apartment to get rid of the bugs, they returned tenfold. Shortly after moving into the apartment, my car gave out. The transmission blew with only 84,000 miles. I wasn't about to be here, in North Carolina, without a functioning car, so I found a dealership down the street from where I was living at the time. God blessed the negotiations and while signing the paperwork, the loan officer at the dealership stated that I could have purchased two vehicles because my credit was so outstanding. I was like "For real! Are you serious?" They said, "Your credit is good enough to get two vehicles."

My first thought was that Othello needed a new vehicle to travel back and forth from Virginia to North Carolina to see his family and take care of business. His current vehicle had a lot of miles on it, and his son also needed a car. I wanted to help. I felt that by being his lady and building a life together, I could help, so at this point, I leased the second vehicle, a Nissan Frontier, for him. And because of his crazy behavior of wanting his cake and eating it too, it became the cause of him losing out.

So, at the end of our relationship, when I took him to court to repair the damage to my credit and release myself from paying for a vehicle I wasn't driving, he had the gall to get mad. What was the point when he caused this himself?

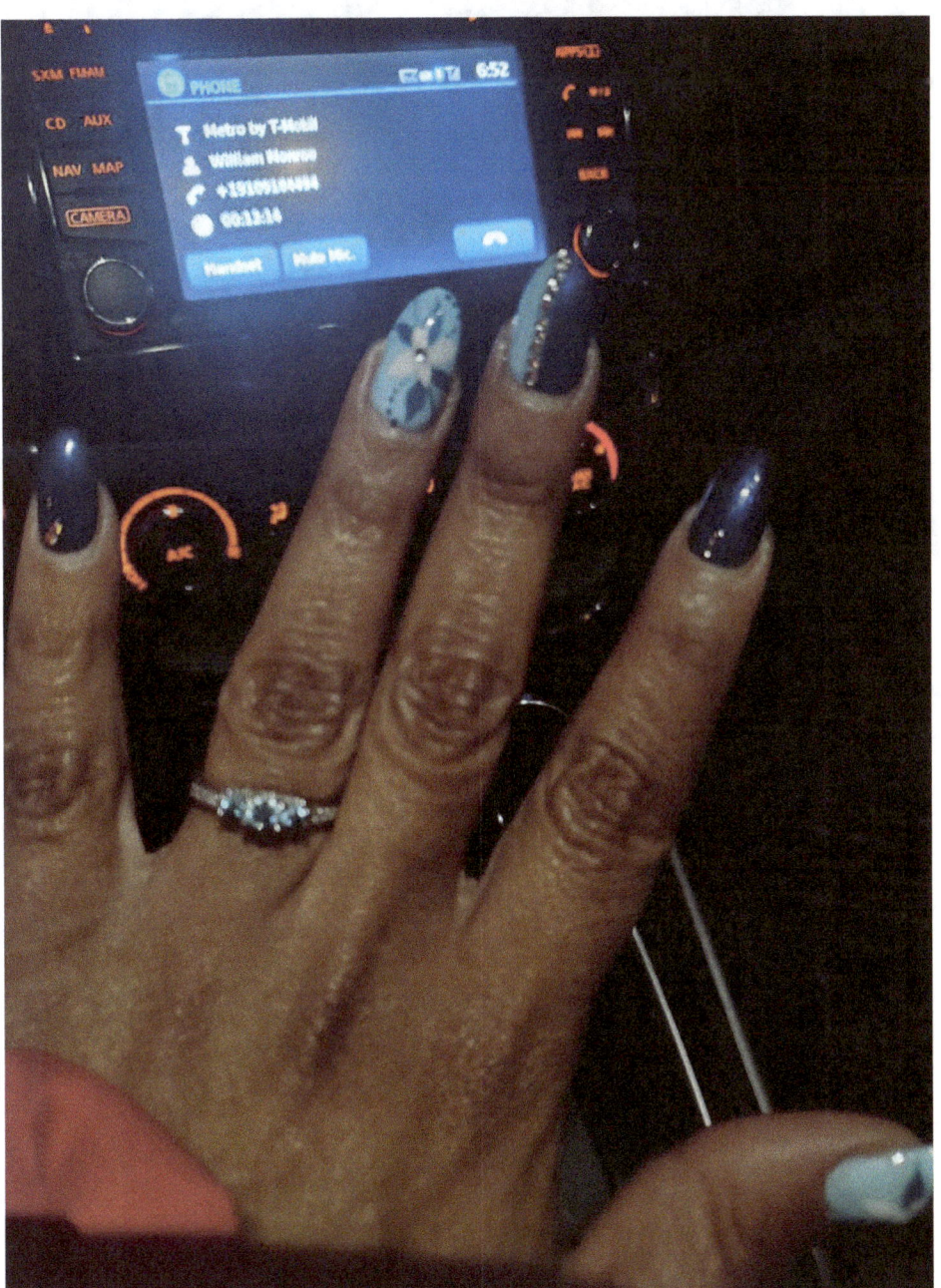

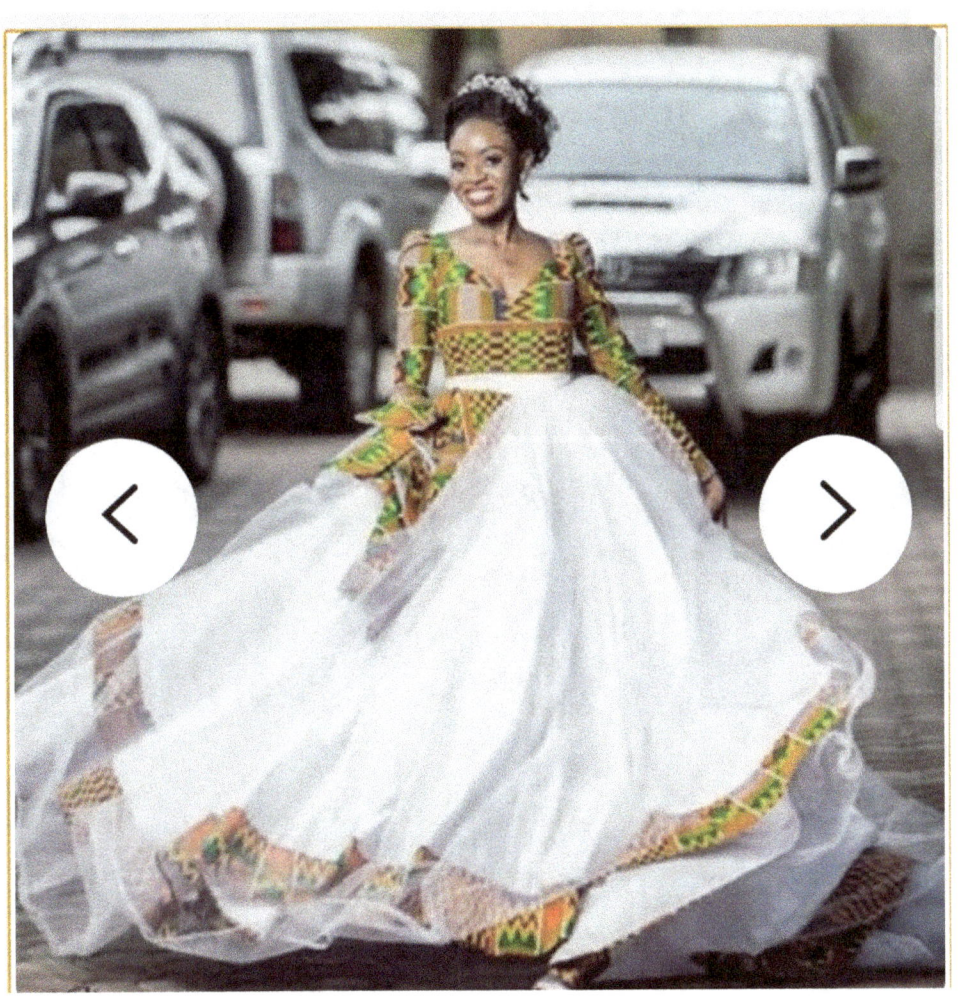

## Chapter 8

## What is Narcissist Behavior

Sensor: Please, people as you read this, prepare yourself mentally for visual effects of what happens to your mind, body, as well as emotions when going through a narcissist relationship.

### *Cycle of Narcissistic Abuse*

The narcissistic abuse cycle refers to an abusive pattern of behavior that characterizes the relationships of people with narcissistic traits. It involves idealizing a person, then devaluing them repeatedly, repeating the cycle, and eventually discarding them when they are useless.

### *Idealization stage.*

The phrase appreciation stage, as it is commonly referred to, typically involves the narcissist love bombing the person, creating a connection that makes them feel unique and one of a kind, allowing the person to feel as if they are the only one. You would say match made in heaven. But they are feeding you beautiful lies as (Yung Bleu and Kehlani) would say. It's romantic, endearing, and friendly, and moves fast to enhance the passion to cover the mask the person hides within. I learned from Dr. Ramani (Durvasula, 2020) that many of us fantasize about what dating, courtship, and love should be based on what we watched on television and films. Charm, charisma, is a way of drawing sensitive individuals. We gauge each other's relationships when we see grandiose gifts and events and compare them to our relationships. When your rose-colored glasses or their pedestal break, you begin to see the cracks, the gaslighting from the narcissist.

    Compliments and gifts are the ones that give you the wow factor, and that can go either way. Gifts can be good or bad depending on the person's mood. I base this thought on my experience. Then you move to an area of spending time together, and the inter-manic is magnetic. It draws you in closer because the passion is being laid on you so thick you think the person is making love to you, but it's them consuming you. Negative energy drains you of what is positive within your soul.

That takes us into the **_Devaluation stage_**. This process starts slow, as if you pull the mask off them and uncover the real person, layer by layer. So, they are dropping hints here and there, and then it becomes everywhere. The indicators are when you see a person being passive-aggressive: excuses for poor behavior (constantly not being accountable for their actions, lying), subtle criticism, stonewalling, mind games, gaslighting, lack of empathy, comparisons to others, ridicule, and humiliation.

With all of this in place, you wonder what is happening. You start to go crazy, or what, because when you allow a person to continue doing such a thing, you allow them to master the craft on you. How long as a collective will we allow these individuals to drain us? It's time for us to free our mind (Tems). It's a mental thing! Once they have what allows your body to keep going, bring understanding, intelligence, etc., it will begin to kill the body as well, and can only be mended through Christ Jesus. So, if the person you're dealing with is not in God, they would not know how to give peace, or the understanding needed to move the relationship forward. And it also must start in the person's heart to manifest in the mind to be produced in the natural, if not pain, bound to come to the surface.

## Repetition Stage

The repetition stage is when you go over and over again to the first two cycles—building you up to break you down all over again, as long as you have something they want. They are all games to keep you in this miserable cycle of ooh, even if it kills (you) me (Melanie Fiona). We would stay because we think it's love! Then, we have the last stage everyone dreads going through, because after you have given your all and everything you have to offer. There is nothing left to give. You are up when you're up (Fat Joe, Remy Ma & French Montana). You are on cloud nine. Like it's you and them against the world, but really, it's just like the good ole (2 Pac) rap, me against the world. And when you're down, lawd, it's hell to pay because the beast has risen. No peace! Not even within. What you say I heard from all of you, Dr. Jekyll and Mr. Hyde, nothing but the blues. The word of God states in Philippians 4:7

*And the peace of God, which passed all understanding, shall keep your hearts.*

When you have nothing left to give, they discard you like you are trash to be picked over like vultures, and they are not going in the dumpster to get you either. They might as well have left you for dead. They want you to feel like you are losing the best thing smoking, and it's all your fault because things ended in the first place. To them, they are the best relationship you ever had, then they hit you with just another *T.K.O* (Teddy Pendergrass) and a little Mike Tyson with a bite to rip off your ear, telling you to sail on like (The Commodores). So, they can continually have their good ole time with someone else, their next victim or prey, you might as well say.

## Chapter 9

## Predicaments

Before moving to North Carolina, I made several trips house hunting. I am fighting internally with myself. Why was I going through repeated pain that I had felt once before. So, woman, you know our intuition. I start to go on a hunt. I called Othello repeatedly getting no answer, no reply through text all night.

During that time, I had no one to talk to, to calm this overwhelming predicament that I was in. So, my decision was to contact his mother and confide in her about my health issues. I cried all night long and began to show signs of post-traumatic stress syndrome (PTSD) breaking down in physical form. My stomach started to hurt I began to vomit. I couldn't eat at all, but the acid of my stomach lining began to consistently come up. Along with having diarrhea as well on a constant basis, it caused my hemorrhoids to expel. As days went by, they got bigger and bigger. I could not sit down at all. My butt felt like pure fire! I was so afraid that everything was becoming a never-ending story. Something had to give! I had to go to the hospital because the pain was unbearable. The doctors ended up puncturing each one to release the buildup of blood that had accumulated.

What a horrible experience to go through emotionally and physically. At this point I still couldn't understand what was going on and how the two were corresponding with one another. All of that happens within a week and a half. I did talk to him maybe thirty minutes after speaking with his mother and it wasn't a pretty conversation at all. He wanted to talk to me over the phone, you know to *make some time* (Bradshaw and Roberson), but I wanted to do a video because I believe you should be able to face someone that you wronged and own your wrongdoings, explain and be genuinely sorry about it and understand and see the hurt in a person to know how they feel as well. But instead, it was *I don't know what you want me to say. You caught me. I'm sorry. I never meant to hurt you. My heart is still open for us to get it right* (Silk Sonic f/Bruno Mars and Anderson. Paak). It was never my intention to do anything to harm you. But the whole time I knew that it was something to say because that is the norm for men when they get caught in the act of wrongdoing. There was no emotion, and he could not look at me. At the point I knew he was a narcissist, but I never had the guts to say anything until the end of the relationship because I had nothing else to lose.

Then when I begin to ask questions and wanted to know details, yes details because I want to know what this woman had that I didn't. What was she doing that I wasn't? What was the importance to take a BIG chance on what we had begun to build? During the explanation he started flipping things on me as if the distance was a problem; time, needs and you can guess how the rest played out. What I gathered from Dr. Ramani (Durvasula, 2024), that with a narcissist they love being argumentative and unrelentless in their goal to win the argument, to break you down. They feel entitled and believe everything should go their way. They use coercive tools to control you and the situation.

Then the gaslighting started and made things even more intense. All the conversations really didn't get anywhere because I could see that it was intentional, and he was doing it the whole time. To contract the bacteria infection three times over the period that we were together. I wasn't good enough to protect him and I guess he wasn't either, it had to be stored in him. I wasn't sleeping with anyone else. And he knew that she was sleeping with other people because he told me. Really? I believed him. I didn't possibly think that maybe he played me again, as he coughed up one indiscretion. I later learned that she and I weren't the only main chicks along with side orders. Can you believe this...

So again, during this sad and depressing conversation, he expresses that he just knew that I was going to break the relationship off because every other woman did when they found out that he stepped out on them. He stated now...Ding, ding ding! Perfect guilt trip and gaslighting again, him playing both the villain and victim. Of course I fell for it.

Things quieted for a moment before there was another pop off moment. It was Thanksgiving. We were all together, and his mother was cooking dinner. The woman could cook, and I was looking forward to the meal and fellowship. Unbeknownst to me, and to this day I still don't know why, my youngest son decided he wanted some cash in his pocket. He takes it out of Othello's mother's purse. A few minutes pass before he thinks better of it and returns the money, only he didn't put the purse back where he found it. Of course, Othello's mother looks for her purse and then accuses my son of stealing. Before he can own up to his mistake, Othello goes ballistic; he and his siblings are just verbally assaulting my son. Me, being mamma bear, I'm standing up for my son. Eventually, the truth does come out. My son apologizes to everyone, but now I'm in my feelings. Up to this point, everything was cool between him and my kids, no issues at all. This left me a little sour.

    For me, I love hard and that can be hard to let go of a person easily, especially when I put time, effort, love and appreciation, sincerity from the beginning without fail. I just would not give up that easily. So here I go again, give him another chance. Here we go again (Isley Brothers). And there you go (Johnny Gill) still playing me like a fiddle.

# Chapter 10

## The Devouring Stage

*Devour – to use up or destroy as if by eating. To prey upon. (Merriam-Webster)*

The only way that you can devour a person is to destroy the spirit and ruin the soul. The word of God states (KJV) Be sober, be vigilant because your adversary, the devil as a roaring lion walketh about, seeking whom he may devour (1 Peter 5:8). But if you read the next verse it says "Whom resist steadfast in the faith, knowing that the same afflictions are accomplished in your brethren that are in the world. Resist him, stand firm in the faith, because you know that the family of believers throughout the world is undergoing the same kind of sufferings. And the God of all grace, who called you to his eternal glory in Christ, after you have suffered a little while, will himself restore you and make you strong and firm, (1 Peter 5:9-10).

I keep thinking about the BBD (Bev Biv Devoe) lyrics, "Tell me when will I see you smile again, cause I know I messed up baby, and you know I feed up sugar." This stage is after all the passion has faded and you are looking for life to go back to being the same from the first moment you meet the person that you fall head over hills for. In this stage you will get put downs, let downs, and fake turn arounds. It may seem as if things are starting to get better, but things hit the fan with arguments, gaslighting which define as psychological manipulation of a person usually over an extended period that causes the victim to question the validity of their own thoughts, perception of reality, or memories and typically leads to confusion, loss of confidence and self-esteem. One becomes uncertain of their emotional or mental stability, and a dependency on the perpetrator.

Perpetrator – the act or practice of grossly misleading someone especially for one's own advantage (Merriam Webster). After all that it caused a person to forget what the point of all this dysfunction of a so-called relationship. It makes no sense to go back and forth for something that you don't understand why it's going on in the first place.

So, in my case, I felt like I had it all with Othello during this time. I felt that he was the missing piece to my puzzle. I was in school for a field of choice I have wanted all my life. Time passes and I was free from years of hurt and wanting to be loved and treated like a woman should be. My children were with me, and we were at peace even though we felt the aftermath from the divorce, it wasn't too much a bother because we just knew that we had Othello as our hero (Mariah Carey). It seems as if he would come in the picture every time we needed to be lifted or saved by grace as people would say. Least we thought that was the case until one day I'm spending time with my children and getting ready for my travels to him.

Within moments I get an inbox Facebook by a woman that knew of him and Margie relationship, Sydney. She comes straight out and asks me "Are you with Cecil?" I never answer because first I didn't know the woman and secondly, I was preparing for my travels to see Othello at the time and then I thought nothing of it because I never called him Cecil. I am not a fan of calling the person I am in a relationship with a short version of a given name unless it's romantic. That is just short of giving them dignity and respect. If that is your given name, I'm going to give you that respect. So, a few days later I get a message again in my Facebook DM from Ms. Margie, and she says that she was in a relationship with Cecil for three years and that she doesn't understand how he is with me because they are engaged.

Of course, you know what I did. I confronted him. At first, he lied and said he didn't know this woman. At this point it didn't sit well with me, so I wasn't going to stop until I got the truth. I called his mother and asked what the deal about this woman was. She also tells me the story that he wasn't involved with her. She doesn't know anything about an engagement or upcoming marriage. I sent pictures that she sent to me, and I said, "Are you sure?" She said, "No!" I should have looked at this as a BIG RED FLAG with him and his mother because they are both liars. Keeping reading. You'll find out why.  But as time went on, he came out with the truth when I stated I was on my way down to Virginia to set this matter straight.

He then sends me this text telling me his feelings, which was nothing but a trick of the mind. We went back and forth at this point because I stated that you need to decide on whom you wanted to be with. I was okay with being dismissed. I had nothing to lose and everything to gain at that point in my life. The pain and suffering weren't worth the dick nor the time that I had to put into the relationship to win him over from any woman. All the love, attention, affection, and the peace that I gave him should have been enough. At least that's what I thought. But when a man wants his cake and eat it too, there is no stopping the itch unless but to scratch it.

    There would be times after that we would fuss, and it would be so crazy. It could be over times to call when we were going to see each other because I wanted to make sure I spent time with him, due to me living in another state. Even when it came down to paying for things that I felt was necessary to have or get at that point of time ideas that were fulfill. OMG the man I felt was crazy and mentally challenged, anyway you want to call it. It was uncalled for and the gaslighting on top of it, just wanting a person to feel that you are what matters. That you are first.

I basically made him my God fully knowing that he would never measure up to the God I served, who I should have been putting first from the start. There was a moment I had to find someone to talk to. It was a 911 (Wyclef Jean f/Mary J. Blige) emergency, and his sister took the call. Good ole Mindy. God used her to the utmost and at that moment I had to look at things for what it was, even if it hurt. Even after that I stayed, but I came into full realization of what I needed to do, until I found a release from the hurt. And it hurt so bad (Whitney Houston).

I should have pumped the breaks and realize that that he was no good for me, and neither was what he put me through just to get a thrill. It all left me in tears. I will never forget the time he called himself dumping me, but he's still talking to me. Plunging me in a hole. I'm feeling like a million pieces of shard glass. That was our relationship, one-sided and broken. Just so he could do what he wanted to do to make himself superior over me. And I took it because I wasn't going to let anything run me off, not even him. I just knew I was a champ. But inside it was breaking me into pieces. And as he was devouring me in every way you could think of, I felt that I had no exit without him being by my side and in my life.

    I made an investment into us and the relationship that I thought that I was building for life. Which it wasn't nothing but to build me up to rip the rug from underneath me. And he didn't even care how he hurt me if he was getting the happiest of what he needs now. Rather it was sex, time, or money. At that point I reconciled that love didn't live here anymore (Rose Royce).

Are you in a relationship with Chris?

APR 27, 2020 AT 1:36 PM

Hello?

APR 27, 2020 AT 2:25 PM

How long and when did you guys start talking?

I heard he's already in a long term relationship with a woman and they've been together a couple years.

MAY 3, 2020 AT 4:03 PM

Look here I m going to say this as nice as I possibly can. I m not interested in what you have to say nor show me .I didn't respond to none of your messages so I m not understanding why do you choose to keep coming into my DM with the information that you choose to share at the end of that you choose to share. At the end of the day there is two sides to a stories . And I get to choose who I want to believe. I know you got my address and I m not going to be looking over my shoulder but best believe I got yours too. So , What I m asking from you is to leave me and Chris alone and keep it moving. Point Blank !

> who I want to believe. I know you got my address and I m not going to be looking over my shoulder but best believe I got yours too. So , What I m asking from you is to leave me and Chris alone and keep it moving. Point Blank ! Basically go about your business. And I will be praying on that.

You can have chris don't message my Fucking phone No more you understand!!!

You got him stop texting me

> You started this shit I never texted u with nothing. That was some childish shit u pull to pop over his house one and then go through his shit

> That's not a real woman

Bitch please

> If I one you one

> Fake ass engagement REALLY pull that shit with a new woman because i m not new to this right here i true to this

MAY 3, 2020 AT 4:29 PM

MAY 3, 2020 AT 4:29 PM

Bitch you fake wtfe enjoy your life because i will enjoy mine with that said stop with the None sense!

It's said you have to look for a Man in Va behind another woman's back.

1. I do want to be with you.
2. I adore you and care for you
3. Asking my why I did it will is rhetorical. I can talk but to be questioned as if I committed a crime with not make me give an answer of of your liking. I regret it happened after the fact. Especially when I realize I do have feelings

Friday, May 1, 2020

There are no words to express what I did other than selfishness and deceit. Yes I was dealing with her, but engaged I WAS NOT! I did not lie to you about the loan or her living in a hotel with her son. I maintained a situation with her so she would not fuck me over with paying the loan I helped he

No Mia. I didn't tell her that. Where did that shit come from. She's a liar. Just like that pic of that ring. That's no engagement ring. But you obviously believe her. So whatever you decide to do, ok.

⭐ 6:16 AM

Look I came clean about everything. Not you decide what you want to do from this point on. I do want

Look I came clean about everything. Not you decide what you want to do from this point on. I do want you in my life but I understand if you don't want to be.

⭐ 6:30 AM

You are a good woman who deserves better than I presented with all this mess. Can I be good to you, YES! But it's up to you to give me a chance to

You are a good woman who deserves better than I presented with all this mess. Can I be good to you, YES! But it's up to you to give me a chance to show you. If it's not in your best interest to deal with me, it's fine. I understand.

⭐ 6:32 AM

Not a problem

Y

O

U

⭐ 6:36 AM

I'm not doing that. Just know I knot going to risk losing you again.

⭐ 6:40 AM

I don't Mia. I didn't want her like that. It was because of the loan and her fulfilling her obligation. I telling the truth. I have hurt too many people in this. And it was for selfless reason. No one deserves to hurt anymore. Now you can accept this or make another decision. But I don't and want pr

## Chapter 11

## Sabbatical

There was a period when I got so tired of feeling the way I did. I felt used, mentally abused, drained, unwanted and misunderstood. It was just a whole joke at this point of the relationship, and I didn't know how to break it off. Not that I want to, but I want him to find out what he wants and whether it was more important than what we had going on with setting down roots. So again, I had a voice – take a sabbatical. I told him that during this time, he would find out what he wanted and needed to make him happy. Because during this time I was fed up with all the cheating and the lies that I was constantly being told.

I never understood why because I always felt that we built a safe place for each other to be open and honest. It would have been much more manageable. And with both of us trying to finish school in our respective fields, we still had other things going on with me having to take exams that I wasn't focused on, but I was tied up and tangled up in Othello, and I just couldn't see anything pass him. At this point, I knew his mind was on other things such as women, so I gave him two sabbatical choices. I felt it would relieve me from everything I was going through with him. And give him time to see what he was doing to us.

The first sabbatical gave him an open invitation, to do whatever he wanted with me out of the picture for a month. And at the end of the month, we could evaluate if we would stay together. Because I felt it was hard for him to be committed to me and only me. He was already scoping and lurking, sexing whomever he wanted to, so why not do that with me in the midst.

It was so hurtful to me, and there were times I begged him, why was he doing this to me and hurting me this way? There were times he laughed about it all. Then he told me days later that it's like putting a broken glass back together, and now it is full of cracks as if I had done him wrong as an excuse to make me feel bad so he could continue doing what he wanted. I wasn't going to continue to go through such things, which is a lost cause of a metaphor, which was already told to me at the beginning of our relationship.

Option number two was to check in with each other at the end of the week. And that was to check on each other, and if doing the week, we decided that this relation wouldn't be beneficial, then we would let it go. The option was put on the table to call if we crossed each other's minds. When the end of the month comes, we will consider what has been going on and where we stand with each other. We should know where our hearts were at that point. But even in this, it was a lot of drama, him fussing off and on calls and the texts. With all that going on, it would trigger my seizures to start acting up. My oh my, the biggest gaslighting ever.

But, at this point I was okay with whatever he picked, because I was done. I didn't think I could take it any longer. But it never happened, he wheeled me back with love bombing. Here I go again; that was all she wrote, sucked back in with me eating out the palm of his hand figuratively speaking, believing that this time would be different. I will be the only woman he's ready to give his heart, soul, and life to.

That monster was a hard thing to shake. He called himself the Hulk and beat his chest; I had the game twisted. I had the beauty in mind, but the beast had already staked his claim. He knew from the jump what he set out to do. It wasn't about love at all. Rude boy (Rihanna) showed up and was on the top of his game.

7:05 AM, Aug 25

I'm not reading this mess! The sabbaticals is not a want for me, it's a NEED! And it's a NEED for you too. It's not an US in this because you imposed it and you think it's the best thing. This shit is new to me. So let me experience this new thing without you constantly nit picking, digging in to, prying for negative information from my text I sent you. I'm using this time to search ME! To make sure my forgiveness of myself is not compromised by guilt and sorrow. So big ups for me.
I deleted that pic because you are just being manipulative in that I'm not evil or being evil. You just want drama and you want to force me to choose the other sabbatical. lol. If you want the other sabbatical to be put in place because you can't STOP with this drama of dissecting text to make them sound bad. I was just

you imposed it and you think it's the best thing. This shit is new to me. So let me experience this new thing without you constantly nit picking, digging in to, prying for negative information from my text I sent you. I'm using this time to search ME! To make sure my forgiveness of myself is not compromised by guilt and sorrow. So big ups for me.

I deleted that pic because you are just being manipulative in that I'm not evil or being evil. You just want drama and you want to force me to choose the other sabbatical. lol. If you want the other sabbatical to be put in place because you can't STOP with this drama of dissecting text to make them sound bad. I was just brief with my text that's alll and you had to make it seem "evil". Now you decide. And stop asking me.

> **Me**
> 7:55 AM, Aug 20

Everytime I try to help us you always think negative ever since I found you out completely. And it's cool. But, you and no one else will get the opportunity to hurt me , mistreat or do wrong by me .
I m to good of woman for that. I basically give you the world that you never ask for. And you mouth and how you think about me is how you feel.

**Me**
8:11 AM, Aug 20

**(No subject)**

conclusion that you feel the need to do ,do it !
Stay or Go
At this point I not forcing you to make changes, I not forcing you to see what a man suppose to do in a relationship soon to be marriage, I m not forcing you to love me nor care for me. I not even forcing you to support my dreams that I have for you or myself.

Basically, 🎵YOU CAN DO WHATEVER YOU LIKE...🎵
Like I Said to you before and time and time again I KNOW MY WORTH and if you don't think you are worthy of me and what you are getting or have gotten or will get STEP.
Not being mean just being real.
I ready for REAL LOVE and that

> **Me**
> 8:26 AM, Aug 20

THIS IS NOT A TEST..
(as the television would say)!!
It's you figuring out what you truly want and what you truly want to be. And how do you want to end up in life at the end of the day.
You think I want this, you are my person, My friend, my partner, my lover.
I can't see life without but, I m not going to be hurt neither.
I give you the upmost respect. You can't say I don't.

I can't see life without but, I m not going to be hurt neither.
I give you the upmost respect. You can't say I don't.
But, every person that comes in your life and that us in your life should know about █████████

Just as we who is in my life or comes in my life should know and does know about ███████████
male or female.
And if you can't do that it's a problem.
If you can't understand what I telling you us a bother for me I don't know what to say

**Me**
10:47 AM, Aug 18

All I know is that you motherfucking azz better NOT hurt me NO fucking more since you feel you got this that you can reschedule some appointment took a long time to even get.
You not dealing with thr hurt I m and just to even know you didn't attend appointment that dealt with it. How the hell I suppose to feel.
If that shoe was on the other foot.
I probably would be every name in the book, dismissed, dog out and then some.
And all I m asking is that you get help and not do this to me again. And treat me like the High Value Woman I m. But, you don't want to hear my mouth and it's something dealing with you all the time that make me say something. Check it out tell me what you got on me to complain about NOT A MOTHER

## Chapter 12

## The Encounter

Feeling sick for a few weeks, both mentally and physically, was causing my body to shut down from all the stress and turmoil that was going on in the relationship. During this time, I tried to go to a few hospitals to find out the cause from a doctor's standpoint. But every time I would go to a hospital in North Carolina, they were full, and the waiting time was excessive.

So, after traveling as far as Durham, North Carolina, I went to a Virginia hospital. I get to Chippenham Hospital. At this point my body was to the point where I couldn't even walk. Are you wondering if he was by my side through this ordeal? Yes, he acted like he wasn't the reason for this madness. The mental took over the physical. And I began to tell myself, Marissa, you shouldn't be overthinking or overdoing. You are just on an overload girl. Chill out.

    Meanwhile, I stayed in the hospital and had so many tests run on me just to find out precisely that my mind had shut down my body. There he, Othello, was taking charge, talking and running his mouth, from when we got to the hospital to when he picked me up. From that point, I felt like I was going backwards downward. Although this time, he would say the harshest things to me, worse than ever. As if I needed that. During this episode, he had to nurse me back to health due to the doctors stating that I needed supervision. Of course I could have my children help me, but why would he put that on them when he was the cause of the affliction to begin with. So, he took me back to his house and waited on me hand and foot. Wow! But no thank you? Fronting like we were *living the good life* (Devon

Gilfillan)—just the opposite. We were two fools patiently waiting for each other to give the last word. Both of us want to be on top of winning a fight. It was like watching the WWF on TV in the new millennium—so much drama with no battle to fight to the match. But I could say that after the doorbell rang. My God, all HELL broke loose.

Odessa is at his front door while I was in the bedroom. Looking back, her unexpected drop-in really wasn't unexpected at all. She had a point to make. Me? I'm having an OMG moment. Is this what we're doing right now? I'm thinking that it's bold of her. Before she rang the bell, Othello asked me if I wanted to meet his next-door neighbor. I said sure that would be no problem. The neighbor knew about me, but we hadn't met yet. I also learned about Odessa from previous conversations before our relationship, but I had never met her in person. So, when the knock came at the door, I'm thinking it's the neighbor. But it's not; it's Odessa calling me as if she had known me for years. I'm asking her, "Like how in the world do you know me and who are you?" She begins ranting, rumbling at the mouth, about their past and how she knows about me.

Suddenly, I began putting two and two together. I comment, "Oh, you are the woman I dreamt about. Look at that." I couldn't tell by the hair because it was natural. She continued, and as she was talking, I asked Othello, "So is she the one you got the bacteria infection from?" It was clear that she heard me. I informed her that I have my doctor's information on my phone and quickly pulled it up for her. She states that she took a test, and her results returned negative. And... boy, Othello couldn't wait to cosign for her on that matter. But indeed, he knew that he was the ONLY ONE! The only one I was dealing with. And the only one I was sleeping with. So, is this the part where you want to accuse me of going outside our relationship? Not saying that the thought didn't cross my mind. But, somehow I knew this was a lesson for me based on how my life had gone.

After they left the room, you couldn't hear anything but fussing, arguing, and a few hits bouncing back and forth. I called his mother to inform her of what just transpired. She tried to talk with him to calm him down, but that wasn't in the cards to work out like I thought it would. Until his son came in to save the day. Crank that (Soulja Boy). It just was a whole hot mess. I wasn't looking forward to the aftermath that's for sure. The Beast came out to make his presence known that night and had no regard for anyone's feelings.

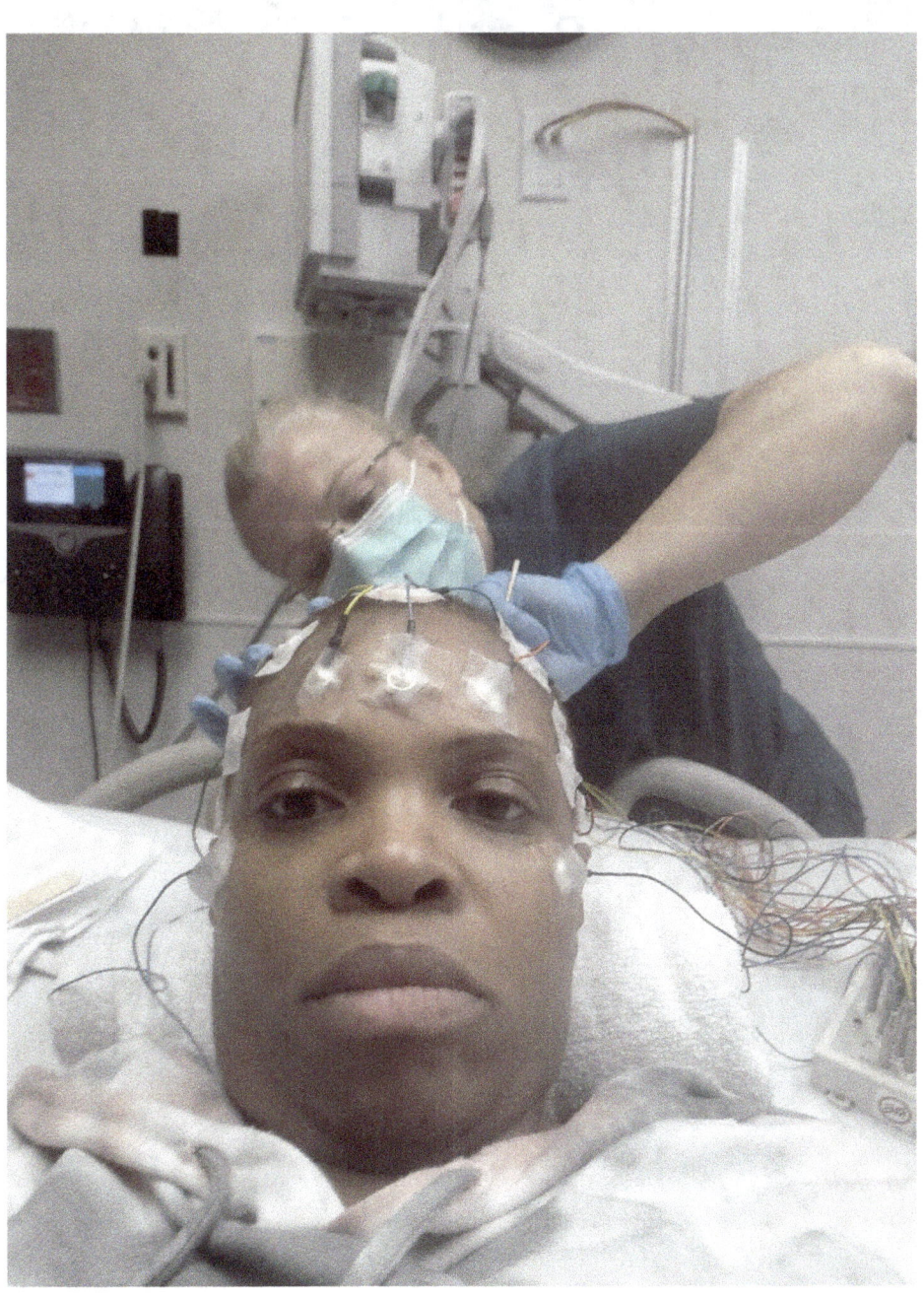

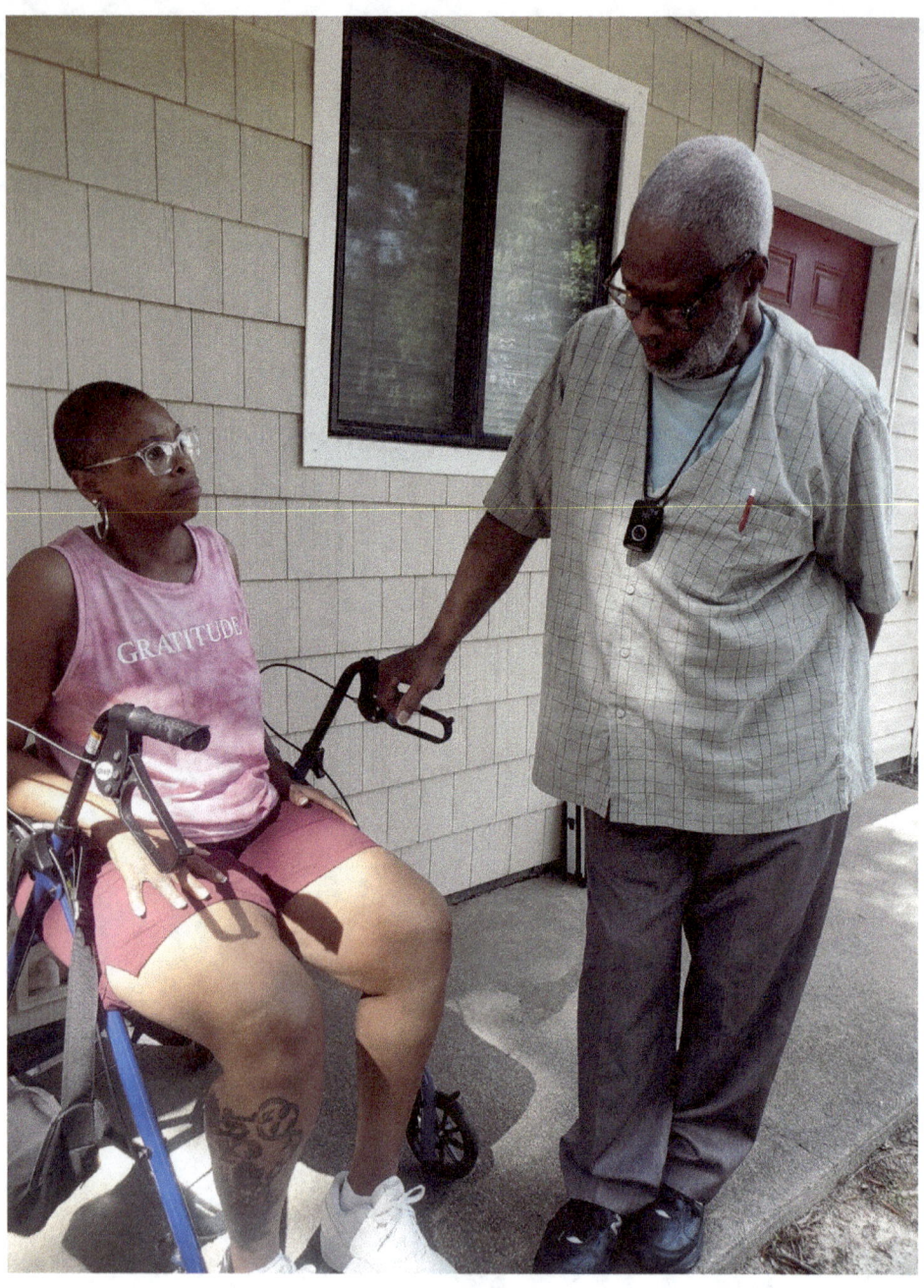

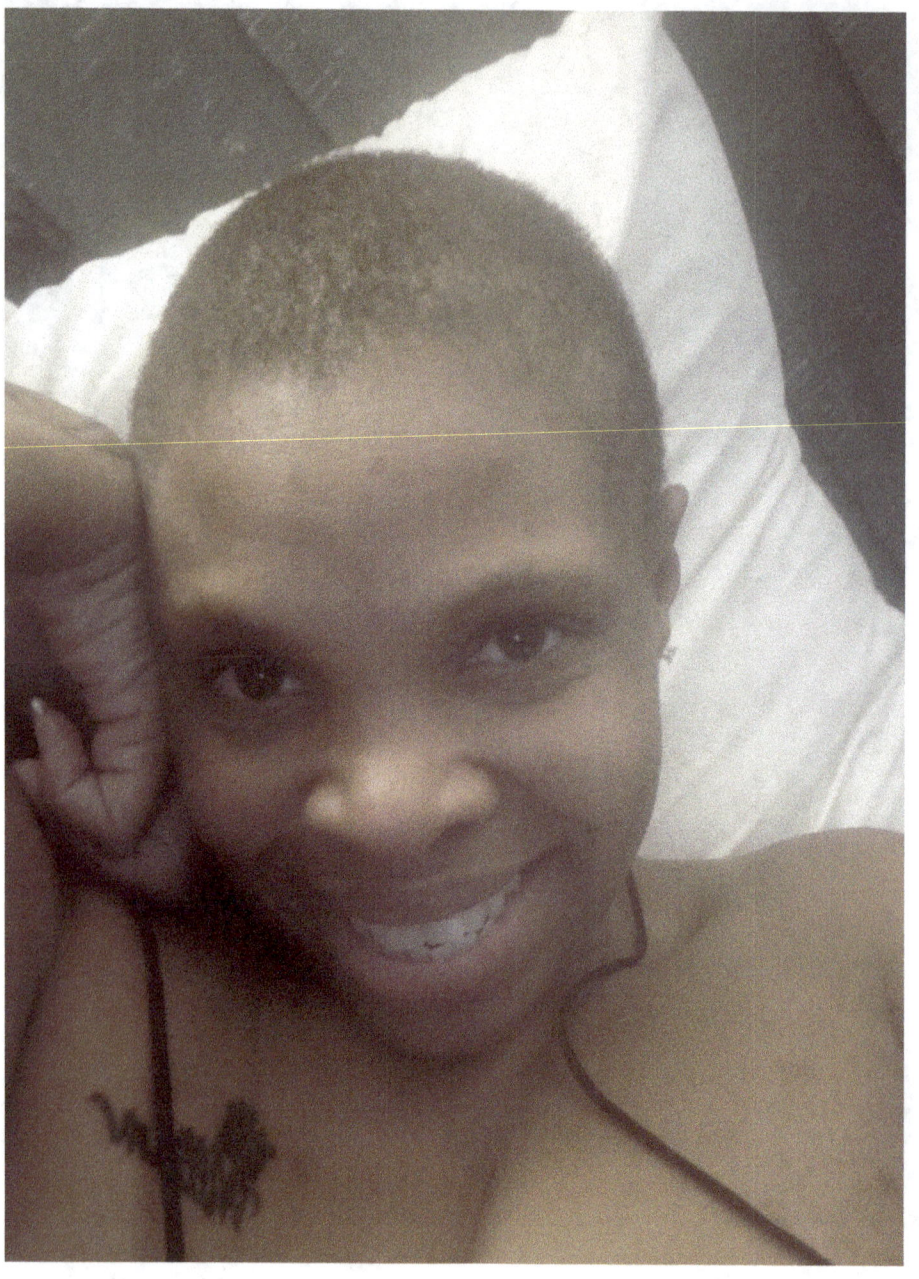

# "Replace funds for using the wrong card and hotel funds"
# - $680

## Social activity

 0     0

---

## Status
Complete

## Payment method
**Visa Debit**
Debit •••• 7476

## Transaction details
June 4, 2021 4:40 PM · 🔒 **Private**

# "Return funds"
# - $400

Social activity

 0      0

---

Status
Complete

Payment method

**VISA** Visa Debit
Debit •••• 2989

Transaction details
May 6, 2022 2:56 AM · 🔒 Private

I was happy you were ok but sadden you were going through this new life you would have to live.   7:57 PM

Delivered 7:58 PM   Ok thxs babe

 I knew I loved you because I worried about you everyday.   8:02 PM

Delivered 8:03 PM   Awe babe 🧡

Seeing you made me feel whole again. The thought of losing you was a living nightmare.   8:03 PM

## Chapter 13

## The Complete End Of The Road

Wow! I had the run in with Odessa and it was through, so I thought, that he broke it off with her, but then her grandmother passed away. She not me, (Chris Brown) and for the life of me, I will never understand the connection. However, me, being the sincere person that I am, was like you had a life before and I am not going to hold you back from giving your condolences to someone you knew and respected. I tell Othello, go ahead, and pay your respects.

Of course, I know the whole play out of a funeral, from the time it starts until every end. This is my livelihood, I studied and worked hard to master my craft working with different funeral homes and directors. I waited ample time for the service to be over before I called Othello to check in. I called and called and called this fool. Hours had gone by. Do you think he called me back? Triple NO! His excuse – "So sorry, ah, I was spending time with her brother and uncle. I spend a lot of time with them when we were together. We were very cool with one another." All I could do was roll my eyes. Like lawd have mercy, this nigga think that I am a fool. Please! I then answer, "ok baby," like it's cool. I got off the phone like he must think I am the dumbest chick on this planet. Not in that way at all but to say I was.

      The final straw was when I put my family in the middle of it. As if it was going to help something that was already disposed of. We were done. We both checked out, but silly me try because I didn't want to feel like I was a failure at LOVE, due to past relationships I have experienced. The relationship was beyond toxic at this point because of him and it wasn't nothing that I could do about it. But my sister talked with him and my brother in-law as well. Being a preacher and all, he provided counsel, but I just believed in my whole heart Othello was playing along. It was a game to him, and it wasn't NO WAY that he was interested especially when he said from the jump I don't believe in God. What a fool I was, but it continued and when Othello talked to my sister his statement was this, *oh she has a soothing voice. If I wanted her, I could have her too.* I'm looking at him and feeling like *boy you are so childish. You done lost your mind* to ever think that you can tell me about some bull like that and me not say a thing. You have another thing coming. So that turns into another big argument, and I wasn't backing down off it either.

During these counseling sessions we were not supposed to be talking about anything afterwards, but I just couldn't help myself. He knew the stuff that he was yakking about had no meaning. It was only to keep me mad and angry. And then he mentions something personal that I exposed about my sister. I thought that it would stay confidential between us, but he used it to add into his lie in denying what he said. He hurt my sister's feelings, but he thought that it was going to destroy me and my sister's relationship. Shame on him! It didn't at all. My brother-in-law Maruice told him straight up, *you come in to destroy something Marissa and Maxine been through. Man, those sisters have been through hell and back. What you did only made their bond stronger. Every time someone tries to come between them, that bond keeps getting stronger. So, no, you didn't do anything at all. And if you think you can get my wife, you can try. You wouldn't be the first. I trust my wife and as a matter of fact, I know she won't give you the time, the day, or even look your way.* My family done what I had been trying to do for months, put him in his place. Othello came across a few lanes just to get thrown back to the curb!

What? I just felt the man had gone bonkers and I was over it. Eventually we did get back together, but what in the world was I thinking? God was giving me an out right there. My lesson wasn't supposed to be long. I chose it to be. Karma (Donnell Jones) chooses you; you don't choose it. Learn the lesson and move on people. Stop holding on to something that you know will not change but will only change you.

In the long run, it made me bitter, angry, upset, mad, ornery, and disappointed. I felt more disabled, unloved, or wanted, unappreciated, walked out and even talked about by him now. I could go on and on with this list, but what good will it do? Only thing that I can say, it will take you to a place of ill will and that is nothing I ever wanted for my life (Donnell Jones). My children were a part of this from day one because they longed for a father figure. When Othello and I first hooked up, their father didn't want to be part of their lives, or mine, for his own personal reasons. That was something that I had to deal with along with what I had going on. And it was okay. I didn't understand then, but I understand now. It was a part of the whole lesson to be learned.

> You didn't read babe. I had to take a test. Why aren't you paying attention to me instead of your own thinking. I'm not you. You keep thinking I'm not competent enough to make a sound decision.

I'm not you. You keep thinking I'm not competent enough to make a sound decision. Especially when it comes to my medical or mental health appointments. Now you have a gmfd!

10:36 AM

**Me**
10:25 AM, Aug 18

But, I start stuff , I wrong
But, like I tell you everything that you desire from me I know 💯 % I give to you. Without a doubt in my mind. But, when it comes to me and what I ask look rescheduled,  let see what I got, I when you go home, don't have expectations. Etc. You not the one that was getting hurt by you action or stuffing I was and that right shows me what more important. Like I said everything but me.

> **Me**
> 10:17 AM, Aug 18

I already know this was going to happen. Why you think I said something to you about the appointment. Replay our conversation in your head. You ask me you don't usually say anything about my other appointment. I said you right. Then you said why am I so concerned and how did you remember because I seen it on your calendar and I said yes. When I looked at it. In my head it read just how it was on your calendar and Big as day MISSED was stamp on it in red.

> Just finished my test on chapter 2 but I missed my appointment. Just letting you know. I called to reschedule. Waiting on the call back.
>
> 9:57 AM

> I am putting everything I have into us ( bills and moving) I am trying really hard not to ask you for anything. I just trying to set my mind on doing what I got to do right now.
>
> Delivered 12:38 PM

> I love you Mia. This is my assurance to you that I'm not going anywhere. No one but you has my attention or my focus. Just you baby!
>
> 4:12 PM

4:44 PM, Aug 6

## (No subject)

You still doing it even though you said you not. Smh. You can't help it. And it's fine. I never told you she was on my mind. You asked me a question and I said , yea she crossed my mind. Then I explained the writing on the mirror. I had my son take a pic of my mirror. The writing is still there.
But you took the shit too far. Then you want to tell me to go be with her. You manipulative behavior is ridiculous. And I'm tired of it. All in? I'm all in but you trying your best to push me out with this mess and other mess. I asked you to listen to me and stop drawing your own conclusions. But now , once again, I'm not there with you and this is what you do in some shape or form. You got to have this kind of

4:44 PM, Aug 6

**(No subject)**

stuff going on where I have to KEEP reassuring you of who I want to be with. Crazy! This is ridiculous when we were together last week and everything to me was perfect and I'm an instance we on this decision crap again because you keep bringing it up. Naw, I made up my mind and I'm done reassuring you. So you make a decision on what you want.

Don't call me with this mess from last night anymore. If you want to break up with me then you will be the one to do it. And lastly, let me say this.... I'm not with you because of what you can do for me. In fact you can stop since that the fucked up way you thinking. I haven't asked you for anything. So you can do

First of all, I did not say that I cheated on you when we argued. I never said that.
The stuff you are talking about in these text were not going talked about at all. No one spoke about you not being a good woman, I never mentioned anything about cheating. You got in your feeling because of the stories I shared. I didn't share them for you to take shots at me about my past or to cause friction between us. You did this in your own head Mia. I didn't say anything to support cheating. Why are you doing this? And you asked me to be honest and this is what I get for it?
And that last text make no sense to me. Who said anything about going back to her? You all fucked up!

6:03 PM, Jul 20

## (No subject)

Being A Protector To You
I know it seems I have left you out from the cover of darkness and maybe even handed you over to the wolves. I wasn't fully aware of what you meant by protecting you. Now I know. I know that not only should I try to protect you from the elements that cause you seizures, but I need to guard you from unnecessary stress, physical hurt, foolery, and anything that disrupts good order and peace for you. I apologize for not doing so those times you were sick. I know it was me and my folly. I admit to it. But I will not put you in jeopardy or any one else again. These are the things I further need to protect you from:
1. Me nonsense

6:03 PM, Jul 20

**(No subject)**

2. No yelling ( unless you are at fault)
3. From cursing at you and sometimes when I'm just talk.
4. Protect you from negative energy or people.
5. Harmful food you like to eat.
6. Too much hallmark tv
7. Not enough naked and afraid.
8. Alcohol abuse
9. Leonard
10. Filth
11. Lifting heavy weight
12. Driving long distances
15. Negative thinking
19. Angry animals
22. Zombies
27. Democratic voting
33. Anything that means us no good !!!!

I didn't say I didn't care about you.
All you have to do is look back. My actions were not all bad. I was there for you. Enough said.
I knew you want to low key argue. And I do care that you are hurting.

9:31 AM

### William Monroe
5:17 PM, Aug 6

Look you can draw wherever conclusions about the past. Im now there anymore. Secondly, what happened to you letting it go from last night ?
What do you want now because I'm tired of this back and forth reassurance and repeating yourself over and over again. So make up yo mind so I can be in peace. What do you want to do? I'm not asking for your patience because I'm not. Of course I said that and I meant it but you got to tie everything to my affair. So be it. What's next for us? I do t want to take it back but if it wasn't given to me out of goodness, yes take it back.

## Chapter 14

## Lessons

Lessons. That's what life really is all about. Souls coming to earth to have a human experience. The understanding of how to raise conscious awareness. And learning right from wrong. Raise the vibration through the energy that we as a people give off. We want to feel the love when a person comes in our present, but it will not always be that way. God will present you options. As humans we make choices to follow His word told us to come unto as a little child or get burnt making our own choices. In the amplified version of the Bible it states, "I assure you and most solemnly say to you, unless you repent [that is, change your inner self-your old way of thinking, live changed lives] and become like children [trusting, humble, and forgiving], you will never enter the kingdom of heaven."

My love for him was always real. I don't think that I have ever loved that hard, in that way, in my life ever. But, when I knew, or got to the point of seeing for my own eyes that we were not on the same page; unequally yoked as the bible states in 2 Corinthians 6:14, *"Do not be unequally yoke together with unbelievers. For what fellowship has righteousness in lawlessness and what communion has light with darkness?"* What I mean by unequally yoke is really not about the belief system from man's terms. It's about whether we want the same things out of life. Do we see the same outlook? Will we have peace and understanding knowing that we will never agree on the same thing, but our disagreements will never come between what we share for one another?

    Othello's statement was that everything was great and the only thing I saw from the relationship was us having a good time. Not wanting a commitment and God wasn't a thought, so because that was what I wanted, and he didn't it wasn't going to work. Looking back, I had plenty of signs not to engage, to get involved with Othello at that point in my life. Hurt, pain and trauma played a big part in our relationship. And honestly, he didn't ever heal from the first heartbreak. And he continues to leave his life as if all women had something up their sleeve and he would never allow his heart to get in too deep anymore. A lot of the relationship I felt was superficial because it was something that the women want or need so because they were needy, he felt that he could help in that capacity he wanted. That's why after every relationship, it's best to heal so others will not pay the price for things or the past. So, when I came along healed and ready to love again, I got caught up with the damaged goods.

    I honestly believe as time went on for me, and now writing this book, he still holds the presence of the man that I saw at first sight, but he just was broken. And not just with women, but unknown life circumstances beyond his control.

    We are who we are by what we are taught and shown. Sometimes God will allow a scenario to continue to replay until we learn the lesson. You can trust and believe that this time, I got it. No repeated Karma (Donnell Jones) here. And when he chose to dissolve the relationship, I chose to pursue rebuilding my life. My heart and mind gave him plenty of chances to find himself along with God, whom he left behind knowing that he needed his guidance. He had no more excuses to give me at this point because it was over.

But, I will never say that he never crossed my mind or desired how life would have turned out with his present. Love was real no matter how it came about. We never know how REAL love will come. We just have to be ready to receive it when it does. Because losing it may just be the worst thing in our lives and never to have it to return to no one the way we expect any way.

    But as Eric Roberson talks about lessons in life and love, my lesson birthed the greatest gift. My ability and desire to trust me first. Love and faith still live in me (Queen Naija). This relationship delivered me. Listen, when God finally penetrated my heart, my soul, the release of wanting a man to deliver me became wisps of smoke disintegrating (Mary J. Blige, Love Lessons) before my eyes. To say that the right man won't ever come along is not my intention, but my calling became crystal clear. All the years of abuse I went through, the trauma I suffered, and my children saw. And it's not just with relationships but childhood as well. Wounds that were suppressed only to make a comeback to be released and it was then God spoke so clearly to me.

I opened my heart and replied teach me Lord. Humble my heart and soul. Center and anchor my spirit back to your word and use me to teach others how to refocus their lives back towards you. And because of these I want to have an impact on people that needed the help from the things and events that I have ever dealt with. I knew how it hurt, and how I dealt with it. There were many times I just needed someone to talk to. And I long for someone just to understand my heart. The battle of loneliness and being misunderstood was the world I came to know until I broke free. In my healing, God placed in my heart to bring forth a vision to birth a ministry called Raging War. It was to honor the warrior within me and the Phoenix that was on the verge to be risen.

## Chapter 15

## And So It Was Ordered - Judgement

After it was all said and done, I wanted Othello to take responsibility for his actions. I will not call them mistakes because he knew the whole time what he did and was doing to me and every female he encountered. I reached my limit, and I couldn't handle it anymore! So, I went to court and filed a lawsuit for pain, suffering and distress, and for repayment of the vehicles that were in both of our names. When he finally left, he tried to leave me bone dry. He left me with destroyed credit. Here I am, starting over once again. Every creditor was calling asking me for money that I didn't have, that I invested in building the family I believed he said that he wanted with me. Wow! Here I was again. I had put all my faith and trust in a man, whose flesh wasn't worthy of me. I wasn't having it. He doesn't just get to walk away and leave me, the scape goat, to pick up the pieces.

I'm in court, on the first case, and everyone that was there through our whole ordeal was there. It wasn't the fact that I wanted the support, it was the truth that I was seeking. No sides to be taking. Wrong is Wrong and Right is Right. His family is going to stick together like glue. But as the saying goes, if one fall in the ditch, they all fall in the ditch. Because they followed along with the dishonesty, I saw them as no different from him. And for that reason, it cleared him from having to pay me for all the suffering he caused. From every event that happened in this book and all the proof I presented in the book. It was still a part of me in pain, full of rage and trying to process all that I went through, that I could not present my case properly. So, he won. HE WON? Wait a minute, what he won?

I'm numb and dumbfounded. There are some things I just didn't understand. Even his mother hurt me to the core that day. What was even the point for her to lie about the money? They both are liars. I'm finding this out while they stood there before a judge under oath and just flat out lied. I knew for a fact that he told her all about the money because she had an entire conversation with me about it.

They both were getting funds. It doesn't pay to have a good heart when you get walked over by spiteful people looking to play victim to get what you want out of someone. Then he had some nerve to tell the judge that he did nothing to me. How he was there for me, how much he adored me, and how he could never do anything in such a manner. Even reading his text messages and letter, the judge instantly knew it was more than what Othello alluded to. The judge says to him, "Yes you gave her something. You did something to this woman." Turning to me, the judge continues. "Miss, my advice to you is to move on. There are just some relationships that are not meant to last when damage of this magnitude is this deep. I wish you luck in your future. I, the judge, declare this case dismissed!"

    Moving on to the second case, I can't say the same result came about because he recorded his name as co-owner and affixed his signature to every item I was suing for repayment on. He was sadly mistaken that day in court when the judge ordered him to pay me the funds due. You think he did? He paid a partial amount and never gave me another dime towards what he owed me. I never even looked back. Even now I know I will never receive another dime. I have moved on. What I lost; I have complete faith that God will restore just what he said he would do. Now that I have sown my seeds, the harvest has arrived. I am walking in my new season.

12:31 PM, Sep 6

Good afternoon, I don't know if I m blocked or not. But, I m contacting in peace. I need something done with the truck and house.
If you don't want to talk to me. That is fine. You can text me. If you don't want to deal with me we can do this in a legal way.
Just let me know how you want to do it and it will be fine by me.
I really didn't want to bother you but things have due dates and I would like to meet them if I can to the best of my ability

Wednesday, September 7

Whenever you want to talk business call me back but anything else I'm not addressing.

6:02 PM

6:18 PM, Sep 7

Unlike you, I haven't gotten over you yet. But knowing how you feel about me now I will eventually. I have thought about you every day. But I'm trying to stay on a good path with God to be a better me. Now, I will agree to the general, but I need a time frame, expiration date, or something. You not going to be me signing my name for new stuff or whatever. So when you ready to talk about THAT, we can talk. All this other stuff , I'm not trying to revisit and I never told your brother in law I didn't want to marry you.

5:36 PM, Sep 10

Your request is not right. I don't have the truck so if I'm going to pay, then I need the truck. The agreement between us was I would pay $300 toward the truck if I'm driving it. But to pay for your car and we not together and pay for a truck somebody else is going drive is not right. Please respond.

**Me**
5:46 PM, Sep 10

Why would I give you a truck to drive and pay anything and we not together? That doesn't make sense. 2. No one is driving the truck but me and I just getting it clean and gas and then it will be sitting until needed. 3. You played me out of the gifts when I knew better from the jump. I stated from the being what it was.
You not going to get good credit off me and we not together. I building you for someone else. No cool. Pay for what you are getting now. Like coming on. I didn't get that benefit why should someone else.
And I asking you please don't go back and forth with me on this. I m hurt enough about all this mess that I been through

10:47 AM, Sep 20

I never intended to hurt you and you know it Mia. I made mistakes and I can't right those wrongs. I pray for restoration for you and me. God's got us both. I'm not angry or feeling any hateful feelings. I know I was out of order and again I'm sorry. This has not been a cake walk for me. I going through a lot.

4:37 PM, Sep 23

So this is the picture you paint for me after all I have done. I took care of you when you were sick, I moved your entire household by myself,
I did so much for you and yours.
Thing between us until you claim I wanted to be with your sister.
I don't think negative of you at all. If you hate me then you always did. I don't hate you.

## Chapter 16

## Rise of the Phoenix

I just woke up one day and just said I really loved this man. My past is my past and I am making room for my new future. I wanted the world to know but most of all, I wanted this man's stamp on my heart (tattooing his name on my chest) to let him know that no man had this place but him. He was a part of me, and I was a part of him. No one could take his place. But I found out the difference at the end. It was nothing but branding and making an imprint on my heart just to break it into pieces. Boy, did that hurt. It left a stain on my heart. But as I stated, life lessons will leave a print by any means necessary, good, or bad or indifferent.

I was absolutely through and done sleeping with the enemy feeding nothing but negativity to my soul. The beast as I would call him because of all the hurt, pain, and torment he put me through. You understand that dehumanizing the narcissist will not help you heal. "The power has to come back to you (Lopes, 2021)." The spiritual definition of narcissist is one who "drains power from others in order to feel powerful in themselves," (Lopes, 2021). They seem like they have themselves together, but their insecurities messes with them being authentic. Being co-dependent gives away their power, sacrificing their own selves for others in the situation and totally lets the narcissist control them. Narcissists gain their power both mentally and spiritually. A narcissist feels hurt, and shocked from the pain you put them through. They will use that insult towards them to convince you to return to them. You must be brave enough to "change the access code" (Hammock, 2023) to your life.

Dealing with the external beast caused a beast to grow and fester inside me. I was drowning in sorrow as well. So much to where I contemplated suicide. Nothing else matters at that point. The damage was done. Everything in my world was threatening to swallow me whole and I had promised myself once before that I would not end up here again. I knew my destiny; I knew my purpose and the Divine knew he designed me to be greater than my current situation. These last lessons from the relationship with Othello caused me pain and harm, but Karma had to assert itself for me to be abundantly blessed.

One day I woke up and decided to call on a warrior for God. She was one whaling woman. Brought me back from the brink of Hell. Her prayers nursed and built me up spiritually. She came to nurture that which had flourished in me. My prayers to God delivered a new light, a new sense of calm and peace. He removed the seeds of anger and sorrow and redeemed me.

Changing the tattoo was a new outlook on life. It was like I tweaked an ingredient in an old recipe, and that fresh taste was refreshing to my spirit and my soul. It was the final removal of him from my mind, body, and spirit. Love doesn't live here anymore (Rose Royce). Redemption! Redemption brought about the rise of the phoenix. From the ashes of the old tattoo, a new symbol arose. I was very specific in what I wanted redemption to symbolize. To the left of redemption is a lady dancing; that's me. Above redemption is the bird that represents my flight, my freedom. The T in redemption symbolizes the cross which Jesus carried to wipe away all my sins.

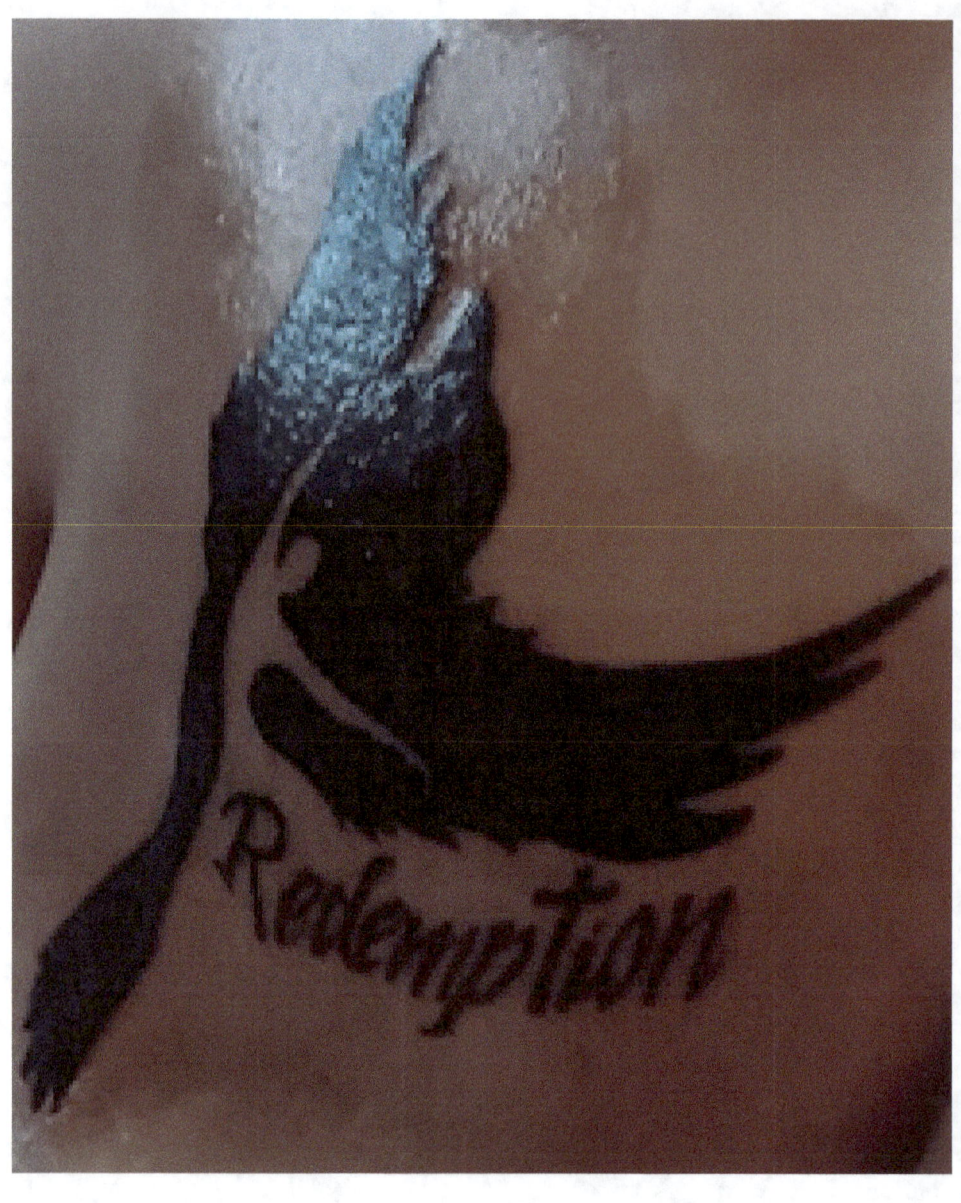

# Chapter 17

## The Birth of Raging War Ministries

Ministry is not new to me. It has been a part of me most of my adult life. I truly believe God created and ordained me to bring positivity and strength to those who struggle in some shape or form in their daily lives. God took every misstep, every joyous triumph and molded His daughter to walk forward with grace, wisdom and the desire to teach and heal wounded souls.

Raging War Ministries is defined as characterized by violent and forceful activity or movement; very intense "a raging battle".

**Scripture**: Psalm 144:1-2

1) Praise be to the Lord my rock, who trains my hands for war, my finger for battle.

2) He is my loving God and my fortress, my stronghold and my deliver, my shield in whom I take refuge, who subdued peoples under me.

**Song**: Teach My Hands to War: Marvin Sapp

**Mission**: That all people have free will to make choices to save and be saved from the dangers of themselves in it or not. We all can be delivered from anything and find refuge in God for he is our haven.

**Focus Points**

**1)** To help people find themselves when put in compromising situations.

**2)** Understand who they are as a person.

3) Help build people self-esteem, confidence, finances, faith, and purpose

4) Spiritual building blocks

5) Help with resources like housing, careers, childcare, self-care etc.

6) Go to different shelters (Men and Women/Children), domestic violence shelters and places to have meetings and reference my book on how to overcome from domestic violence, toxic relationships, and narcissism.

7) Help people who divorce how to get back on track, mentally, physically, financially, and spiritually.

8) Show people how to become whole again starting the transition and getting to the promise.

# Chapter 18

## Discovery

For one night only, the Brian Mcknight 4!
Sat, April 29 8pm
GET YOUR TICKETS NOW!
🎟️ bethesdabluesjazz.com

## THIS IS YOUR TICKET

**STRATHMORE**

| TIME | DATE | ORDER # |
|---|---|---|
| 8:00 PM | Sat, April 11, 2020 | 2070071 |

| SECTION | | SEAT |
|---|---|---|
| ORCH CTR | Brian McKnight | 111 |

| ROW | | |
|---|---|---|
| L | | |

| SEAT | NAME | PRICE | ROW |
|---|---|---|---|
| 111 | Ginny Garayta | $77.00 | L |

CONSTITUENT NUMBER: 509055
TICKET #: 2496418
9900000201497564 7618
SECTION: ORCH CTR

---

# STRATHMORE

**CONTACT US**
Ticket Office: 301.581.5100
Group Sales: 301.581.5199
MD Relay: 800.735.2258
Tea Reservations: 301.581.5108
Administration: 301.581.5200
Mansion Reception: 301.581.5109
Strathmore Stars: 301.581.5145

Music Center at Strathmore
5301 Tuckerman Lane, North Bethesda, MD 20852

Mansion at Strathmore
10701 Rockville Pike, North Bethesda, MD 20852

Directions, parking, and dining information at
www.strathmore.org/visit

NO REFUNDS WILL BE ISSUED. See www.strathmore.org for exchange information. Strathmore's ticket office can only reprint tickets for the original ticket buyer with proof of identification.

ADMISSION POLICY: You are admitted on the condition, and by your use of your ticket you agree, that you will not transmit or aid in transmitting any description, account, picture, or reproduction of the event to which your ticket admits you. By use of your ticket you consent to use of your image or likeness incidental to any live or recorded video display or other transmission or reproduction of the event this ticket admits you to. You also consent to comply with all House Rules. Violation of House Rules or Regulations can result in removal from the event, revocation of your ticket without the refund of any portion of the ticket price, and prosecution. In using your ticket, you assume all risks incidental to the event to which your ticket admits you and waive any rights against Strathmore, the issuer, its agents, management and employees, and performers which you may have arising out of any accident, personal injury, or loss or damage to property. All patrons, regardless of age, must have a ticket. Strathmore Management has the right to refuse admission to any patron for all public ticketed events at Strathmore. Policies, event date, artist, time, program, schedule, and price are subject to change without notice. Strathmore Hall Foundation is a 501(c)(3) nonprofit organization.

---

---

## THIS IS YOUR TICKET

**STRATHMORE**

| TIME | DATE | ORDER # |
|---|---|---|
| 8:00 PM | Sat, April 11, 2020 | 2070071 |

| SECTION | | SEAT |
|---|---|---|
| ORCH CTR | Brian McKnight | 110 |

| ROW | | |
|---|---|---|
| L | | |

| SEAT | NAME | PRICE | ROW |
|---|---|---|---|
| 110 | Ginny Garayta | $77.00 | L |

CONSTITUENT NUMBER: 509055
TICKET #: 2496419
9900000201497564 7619
SECTION: ORCH CTR

---

# STRATHMORE

**CONTACT US**
Ticket Office: 301.581.5100
Group Sales: 301.581.5199
MD Relay: 800.735.2258
Tea Reservations: 301.581.5108
Administration: 301.581.5200
Mansion Reception: 301.581.5109
Strathmore Stars: 301.581.5145

Music Center at Strathmore
5301 Tuckerman Lane, North Bethesda, MD 20852

Mansion at Strathmore
10701 Rockville Pike, North Bethesda, MD 20852

Directions, parking, and dining information at
www.strathmore.org/visit

NO REFUNDS WILL BE ISSUED. See www.strathmore.org for exchange information. Strathmore's ticket office can only reprint tickets for the original ticket buyer with proof of identification.

ADMISSION POLICY: You are admitted on the condition, and by your use of your ticket you agree, that you will not transmit or aid in transmitting any description, account, picture, or reproduction of the event to which your ticket admits you. By use of your ticket you consent to use of your image or likeness incidental to any live or recorded video display or other transmission or reproduction of the event this ticket admits you to. You also consent to comply with all House Rules. Violation of House Rules or Regulations can result in removal from the event, revocation of your ticket without the refund of any portion of the ticket price, and prosecution. In using your ticket, you assume all risks incidental to the event to which your ticket admits you and waive any rights against Strathmore, the issuer, its agents, management and employees, and performers which you may have arising out of any accident, personal injury, or loss or damage to property. All patrons, regardless of age, must have a ticket. Strathmore Management has the right to refuse admission to any patron for all public ticketed events at Strathmore. Policies, event date, artist, time, program, schedule, and price are subject to change without notice. Strathmore Hall Foundation is a 501(c)(3) nonprofit organization.

When I first got into a pure relationship with Othello, healed with no baggage from my past. It didn't matter how we met or even got involved with one another, I knew it was a purpose behind this at this point in my life. It wasn't fleeting passion, nor was it was of attraction. But, it was soul to soul in recognition.

So, I began to place acronyms behind my name. Starting with *walking in purpose*, and as I moved along, I felt it was moving into something else *purpose driven*. I never understood the way it was until later as if my gifts were developing in stages. It just a feeling that this is purposeful and meaningful in some type of way. Not knowing that it would be evolutionary and advanced to my soul. When I was in the relationship there were so many points that I understood the meaning and tried to hold one to something that I knew was a point that I had to let go to be reborn. When ties where cut, the tearing away was as my soul was going through a transformation that I couldn't believe was possible.

I had my fair share of wanting to give up, and at this point life was just too much for me. But then I begin taking life one day at a time. And then I knew that there were people, places and things that I had to shut down, let go and cut off. Meaning no contact. And Othello was one. It taught me how to detach, have compassion, learn how to love by not receiving it in return, having forgiveness regardless of the issue. Now, I am human, so it still goes through a process, but I don't hold it for long periods of time. I don't let what people do to me define how I will treat them. But there were other things that I have learned which are having boundaries not allowing people to do anything that they want to me and think that its ok and I'm going to allow it.

    I also learned reciprocity and that this world was founded on it. It's nothing but give and take with that in return. Whether I give you money and you give me a smile with a thank you, or you pick me up from the airport and I put gas in your car. No matter how reciprocity is, do it with love and allow it to be heart felt not because you feel that you will get something in return. Plain and simple that is called using. And that I had a lot of people that did that in my life, which I never understood that part because I give out the kindness of my heart. If I got it, or I know it's a need, I am doing it with no thought about it. What God bless me with; I don't call it my own. I do what is necessary to do with the funds for me and I hold for God's people. I honestly trust the firm guidelines of what God needs from me, and I have learned to go with the flow which works very well. Peace is what I desire, peace is what I have, and peace is what I will keep. Regardless of circumstances, I know that it will be working out. Spirituality gave me a great understanding what I am here for, my purpose. I meditate and I affirm myself. I allow myself to gain a great deal of love for myself. I started to believe in myself and began to validate myself and not worry about what other people say or think. Learning how to say no to things that doesn't mean me any good. Loving from a distance I learned was fine. I had to honestly say what I meant and stand on it. Because I always felt I was taken for granted.

But here's the thing about love. We come into it knowing what our flaws and weaknesses are. The mate that you chose to engage with, you are discovering things they wish to share; things you slowly uncover and secrets that you may never know. Othello had his demons too. In trying to protect his masculinity and prove that he was not only a protector and provider, he did at times, but it always came at a cost. I saw a lot of solid strengths and then there was the disrespectful behavior that I'll quantify as stank. Some things he masked well and others he fell short. Men are taught from birth to be strong and show few emotions. This caused problems for us as he didn't or couldn't relate to being vulnerable and showing emotional support when I really needed it. His difficulty in fully trusting our relationship to evolve from a superficial arrangement to a true family was significantly influenced by his fear of inadequacy and unresolved emotional trauma stemming from past experiences with family and friends. Rarely would he show his softer side, and when he did, he wrestled with it. I finally came to realize that I wasn't the woman that he would truly change for.

Within a two-year span of time, I learned that if love is real and true it will never die. You must see it in a different light and a different capacity. And that is choosing me. When no one else does you should always choose you. And trust when you love you, there is nothing that can hold you back from what is before you. Know then that the involvement was well worth it. And know that what is meant to will be. You don't have to chase nor fight for something that was yours from the start. If they can't see you for who you are, flaws and all, and understand that love is a choice to do with not wanting the person to be perfect, but just right and just right for you. No matter how many wrongs, know that you must see the person at the end, knowing through it all you will come out being the winner at the end. Always remember sometimes pain is to gain something great and treasure. And therefore, it will always be worth the wait. Ultimately the journey of my pain turned into my bundle of joy.

There's a saying that when a person shows you who they are, believe it. And most of the time it's true. Yet, I also believe that if you truly care about someone, you will put in the work to change behaviors in you that are unpleasing to the other. Commitments are hard work to maintain and requires hard work on both individuals to find a balance that works in harmony. 666....The Beast That Lays Within is a mouthful. I unpacked a lot of hurt, distrust and miscommunication. A lot of you will assume that Othello is the beast, but guess what, so was I. I never looked at myself and asked why did I allow him to continue to do these things to me, knowing then and now in retrospect that it was wrong. I came to realize that all I was seeking was to recover from the hurt and pain from past relationships. I thought I had healed from past relationships, but I found myself right back in an emotional rollercoaster thinking that a man was what I needed to feel true, unconditional love. That love that I so desperately craved from someone else, I finally realized that I had it in me all along. So yes, 666 is what you see it as. I was marked by the beast on every level, physically, emotionally, mentally and spiritually. Now I know and believe that 6 represents harmony within a partnership; 6 represents balance in every area of my life; and 6 is self-love. I am coming into the most authentic version of me who doesn't need to be liked, wanted or validated from anyone but herself.

**The End.**

## References

Durvasula. (2020, April 2). *What is "love-bombing"? (Glossary of Narcissistic Relationships)*. [Video]. YouTube. https://www.youtube.com/watch?v=WhILcuoVhgE

Durvasula. (2024, January 13). *When narcissism is weaponized by the narcissist*. [Video]. YouTube. https://www.youtube.com/watch?v=c5MRyoAPLMI

Hammock. (2023, August 17). How do narcissists feel when you finally walk away | The Narcissists' Code Ep 828. [Video]. YouTube. https://www.youtube.com/watch?v=-Y5hmOhHFxk

Lopes. (2021, March 9). What's CODEPENDENCY and How to Heal It Quickly! [4 Steps]. [Video]. YouTube. https://www.youtube.com/watch?v=1zIUEo965l8

Lopes. (2021, March 16). What's A NARCISSIST and Why Sensitives Attract Them! [How to Heal]. [Video]. YouTube. https://www.youtube.com/watch?v=lTHvE53uT48

## About the Author

Mia Jones was born and raised in the Charm City of Baltimore, Maryland. *666 The Beast That Lies Within* is her second novel. Her debut novel, *Entangled in Domesticated Love*, chronicles her eleven-year harrowing ordeal at the hands of a domestic abuser.

Finding the strength to rebuild her life, Mia is the creative voice behind Raging War Ministries, now Divine Due Diligence. Divine Due Diligence provides resources for men and women to rebuild their lives from traumatic divorce, domestic abusers. Ms. Jones is available for speaking engagements on domestic violence and overcoming insurmountable odds.

To contact Ms. Jones to schedule a speaking engagement, you can send an email or visit her website.

Email: missioninaction228@gmail.com

Platforms that Ms. Jones are located on are TikTok, Facebook and Instagram.